BOMBS AWAY!

I0458878

A Wood Dragon Book

OTHER BOOKS BY M.G. BUCHOLTZ

FINANCIAL MARKETS

Stock Market Forecasting: *The McWhirter Method De-Mystified*

The Bull, The Bear, and the Planets: *Trading the Financial Markets Using Astrology*

The Lost Science: *Esoteric Math and Astrology Techniques for the Market Trader*

The Cosmic Clock: *Timing the Financial Markets Using Astrology*

Financial Astrology Almanac 2025: *Trading & Investing Using the Planets (12th edition)*

Follow The Trend: *When to Buy and When to Sell*

SCIENCE

The Recipe: *Reviving the Lost Art of Home Distilling*

Field to Flask: *The Fundamentals of Small Batch Distilling (5th Edition)*

Frozen Fury: *Agricultural Crops and Hail Damage*

POLITICS AND SOCIAL ISSUES

Thatcher versus Douglas: *The CCF, the Liberals, and the Mossbank Debate of 1957*

BOMBS AWAY!

HITLER, WORLD WAR II, AND CANADA'S RESPONSE TO THE CRISIS

BY

M.G. BUCHOLTZ, B.SC., MBA, M.SC.

A Wood Dragon Book

BOMBS AWAY!
HITLER, WORLD WAR II, AND CANADA'S RESPONSE TO THE CRISIS

Copyright © 2025 M.G. Bucholtz

The cover of this book shows the image of the Canadian flag with its maple leaf icon to underscore the strong Canadian theme in this book. Strictly speaking, at the time of World War II, Canada was flying the Union Jack as its flag.

The image at the start of each chapter depicts an aircraft towing an object behind. This object is called a *drogue* and was used in aerial gunnery training.

Published by:
Wood Dragon Books
Box 429, Mossbank, Saskatchewan, Canada, S0H 3G0
http://www.wooddragonbooks.com

Cover design by: Callum Jagger/Hyperlight Artwork
Inside Design by: Christine Lee

ISBN: 978-1-990863-89-9 (Paperback)
ISBN : 978-1-990863-91-2 (eBook)
ISBN : 978-1-990863-90-5 (Hardcover)

To contact the writer: supercyclereport@gmail.com

FOREWORD

The Mossbank No.2 Bombing and Gunnery School (1940 to 1944) significantly influenced the outcome of WW II. Today, this facility no longer exists; the people who still have memories of it are few in number. The construction and operation of this facility should be an enduring reminder that Canadians are capable of amazing accomplishments when confronted with a crisis. This remarkable chapter in Canadian history cannot be allowed to fade away.

LIST OF ABBREVIATIONS

AW - Airwoman
AO - Air Observer
BCATP - British Commonwealth Air Training Plan
BGS - Bombing and Gunnery School
C.A.S - Chief of Air Staff
C.O. - Commanding Officer
CPL - Corporal
EFTS - Elementary Flight Training School
F/L - Flight Lieutenant
F/O - Flight Officer
F/Sgt - Flight Sergeant
G/C - Group Captain
GIS - Ground Instruction School
HQ - Headquarters
LAC - Leading Aircraftman
LAW - Leading Airwoman
NCO - Non-Commissioned Officer
N/S - Nursing Seargent
R.A.F - Royal (British) Air Force
RCAF - Royal Canadian Air Force
T.C. - Training and Command
WAG - Wireless Operator Air Gunner
W/C - Wing Commander

CONTENTS

INTRODUCTION

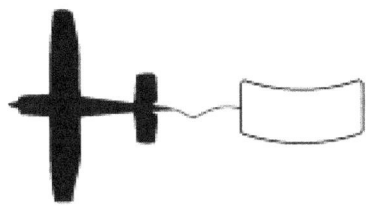

In late 2023, I was approached by two Mossbank businessmen who asked whether I had ever given thought to penning a book about the air training base that had existed near Mossbank in the early 1940s. I knew there had been an airbase near Mossbank during the war, however the details were unknown to me. My knowledge of wartime history in general was sorely lacking, so I wasn't initially caught up with the idea of writing a book on the topic.

Their question lingered in my mind well into 2024. I eventually contacted Jeremy Patzer, Member of Parliament for Cypress Hills – Grasslands, who graciously had his Ottawa staff source some historical articles concerning the airbase. As I read this material in the late summer of 2024, I realized there was a larger story to be told. Motivated to learn more, I began amassing further research material.

In elementary-school history class, I had been taught that World War I was the result of a single event – the shooting of the Archduke of Austria. I had been taught that the cause of World War II was the result of a single event – the 1939 German invasion of Poland. As I began to explore the research material I had amassed for this book project, I came to realize that the causes of both wars were far deeper and more nuanced than what my history teachers had suggested.

As the 1900s dawned, much of the globe was dominated by the British empire, the French empire, the Austo-Hungarian empire, and the Ottoman empire. These colonial masters were well aware that they were sitting atop a house of cards. What they did not know was that their colonial mindset was on the cusp of a severe challenge. Gunshots in Sarajevo sent this house of cards tumbling. As nation turned against nation, the world descended into all-out war. Between 1914 and 1918, over 15 million military personnel and civilians needlessly lost their lives in what the history books now refer to as World War I; the Great War; the war to end all wars.

The geopolitical aftermath of World War I laid the fragile framework for what would be another global conflict twenty years later. Enmeshed in this framework was a hate-filled, anti-Semitic radical by the name of Adolf Hitler. He advanced his agenda practically unchallenged; the hope among European aristocracy and political leaders was that he would fade from the political scene thus eliminating any need for armed conflict. The attitude in Canada expressed by Prime Minister McKenzie King and his Liberal Party was similar. However, go away, Adolf Hitler did not. Finally, in 1939, France and Britain declared war on Germany in response to its incursion into Poland. Canada followed suit in a show of support for Mother Britain.

Britain's realization that it was ill-equipped to defend itself quickly led to Canada playing a role in providing trained pilots, navigators, gunners, and bomb aimers to the British Royal Air Force (RAF). This training program was called the British Commonwealth Air Training Plan (BCATP). The Plan divided Canada into four Training Command zones. Each zone had Initial Flight Training Schools, Air Observer Schools, Navigation Schools, Wireless Schools, Operational Training Units, and Bombing and Gunnery Schools. In total, there were over 55 facilities from coast to coast. One of the locations selected to operate under No. 4 Training Command was situated just outside the small farming community of Mossbank, Saskatchewan. This site was called the Mossbank No.2 Bombing and Gunnery School.

This book is partly a commentary on European political history (1918-1944), which hopefully will broaden the reader's perspective of the interconnected political economy that spanned the years between World War I and II. This book is also partly a commentary on Canadian political history (1937-1944), which will give the reader insight into the attitude of Prime Minister McKenzie King which shaped the Canadian response to Adolf Hitler and his campaign of aggression in Europe.

This book is also a description of the Mossbank No.2 Bombing and Gunnery School that operated between 1940 and 1944. One valuable piece of material that was obtained while researching this book was a copy of the Commanding Officer's daily logbook. Quotes from the logbook are combined with photographs obtained from Archives Saskatchewan to help create in the reader's mind a vivid sense of what life might have been like at the Mossbank No.2 Bombing and Gunnery School.

Throughout this book, the reader might detect some parallels between the events leading up to World War II and the curent geopolitical policy emanating from Washington. As I wrote this book, the global geopolitical tensions reverberating around the world made me pause many times to reflect on an important question: Could a widespread global conflict ever arise again? The short answer, regrettably, is "Yes".

I hope that this book finds its way into the hands of those who are enamoured with wartime history. I also hope this book finds its way into the hands of local people in the Mossbank area. The story of the Mossbank No.2 Bombing and Gunnery School serves as a reminder that Canadians are very capable of rising to meet a threat whether that threat is a hostile foreign nation or a nation intent on a trade dispute. I further hope it finds its way into the hands of educators who shape the minds and attitudes of the next generation of citizens. The period of world history from 1918 to 1944 is a reminder that we must all strive for tolerance and moderation when interacting with our fellow man. We must set aside our differences. History cannot be allowed to repeat itself.

HOUSE OF CARDS

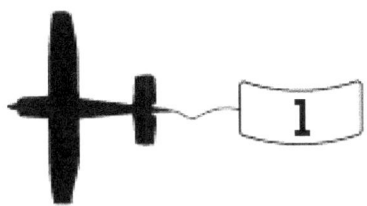

The trigger for the start of World War I traces its origins to the geopolitical structure of the world at the dawn of the new century in 1900.

THE PEAK OF COLONIZATION

The final years of the 1800s marked the peak of expansionist, colonial ideology; the peak of Empire. Britain and France were the two most powerful nations on the planet. The British had colonized nearly one-quarter of the world and held political and economic sway over some 450 million people. The French had colonized large parts of: Africa, the Middle East, and south-east Asia. The Habsburg empire (Austro-Hungarian empire) held influence over parts of: Bosnia, Herzegovina, Croatia, Slovenia, the Czech Republic, Slovakia,

Hungary, Italy, Poland, Rumania, Serbia, and Ukraine. The Ottoman empire controlled parts of: Turkey, Greece, Bulgaria, Egypt, Hungary, Macedonia, Rumania, Bosnia, and Herzegovina.

Germany was the dominant economic and manufacturing power in Europe and had used its wealth and power to pursue colonialization as well. Parts of present-day Burundi, Rwanda, Tanzania, Namibia, Cameroon, Gabon, Congo, Central African Republic, Chad, Nigeria, Togo, and Ghana were under German control. The German reach even extended into the Pacific region where New Guinea, Nauru, and Samoa were under German control.

Although Russia was not a dominant power, it did harbor expansionist desires. Since the late 1600s, Russia had engaged in skirmishes with what it regarded as a weakening Ottoman empire. In 1878, at the conclusion of yet another conflict, France, Britain, and the Austro-Hungarian empire insisted that Russia submit to signing the *Treaty of Berlin*. The focus of this treaty was the Balkan region of eastern Europe. The Treaty made Serbia an independent state and also reorganized the Balkan region giving the Austo-Hungarian empire control over parts of Bosnia and Herzegovina. The Ottoman empire was allowed to retain control over other parts of Bosnia and Herzegovina. Russia was shut out of the global control game, but not permanently. It eventually began building a relationship with France and by 1894, relations between the two countries were strong enough that they signed the *Franco-Russian Alliance*. Germany viewed this alliance with unease and the German Kaiser began quietly laying plans for an eventual war with the two of them.

Four significant colonial mindsets plus Russia plus Germany all attempting to co-exist was an unstable, unsustainable recipe. It was, by any other description, a house of cards.

COMPLEX ALLIANCES

The start of the new century would shake the house of cards. In 1900, the British empire stood strong and tall. But an ill-conceived military strategy would soon undermine this strength. The discovery of gold in the British-influenced Transvaal and Orange Free State parts of southern Africa brought an influx of British fortune-seekers into the area. This influx created tensions with the local population. Britain responded by sending troops into the region. Over the next two years, the situation spiraled out of control resulting in the British adopting aggressive tactics including the creation of concentration camps. The British eventually succeeded in taking control of the area but Britain's popularity, strength, and prestige on the world stage were all badly damaged. European leaders were now reticent to form alliances with Britain. The house of cards had been shaken indeed.

The *Treaty of Berlin* was upended on October 6, 1908 when Austro-Hungarian emperor Franz Joseph I bluntly informed the Ottoman Empire that he was annexing Bosnia and Herzegovina territory that was under Ottoman control. This bold move was a tipping point. It set the stage for the formation of a series of alliances between nations vowing to support one another in the event of further territorial aggression. Russia and Serbia agreed to support one another; France and Russia agreed to continued mutual support; Germany, Italy, and Austro-Hungary all agreed to look out for each other; Britain, France, and Belgium inked a deal; France, Britain, and Russia agreed to a pact; Japan and Britain agreed to an alignment; and Turkey agreed to support Germany in the event that Germany acted against Russia. The house of cards had been shaken again.

As relations between nations grew more complex, Germany sensed that these alliances would ultimately prove unstable. The German Kaiser, Wilhelm II (a grandson of Queen Victoria), decided that when these alliances were eventually put to the test, Germany could either play the role of the hammer or the anvil; it could either do the hitting, or it could be hit upon. He decided Germany would be the hammer. To prepare for this role, he assessed Germany's military strengths and decided that what Germany needed was a strong navy. He began to solicit support amongst politicians in the German parliament (Reichstag) for budgetary approvals to fund a program of naval expansion. At one point, in order to garner support from the minority Conservative Party (the DKP), who supported farmers, the Kaiser enacted a steep tariff on Russian agricultural imports. This ensured him the votes he needed in the Reichstag. However, this gambit had consequences: Russia was incensed.

In the years leading up to 1908, the British Navy ruled the high seas. Britain expressed disdain at the German naval expansion efforts and relations between the two nations dimmed. The house of cards had been shaken yet again.

TIPPING POINT: SARAJEVO 1914

Although the *Treaty of Berlin* had made Serbia an independent state in 1878, the people of Serbia had a grudge to bear. They felt that people of Serbian heritage living within the borders of the Austro-Hungarian empire were "under occupation." Antagonism between Serbia and the Austro-Hungarian empire began to ferment.

This antagonism reached a tipping point in Sarajevo (the capital of Bosnia) in June 1914 when a Serbian radical by the name of Gavrilo Princip fired shots into the open motorcade of Archduke Franz Ferdinand of Austria who had come to Sarajevo to inspect troops from the recently annexed Bosnia and Herzegovina region. In the aftermath of this attack, both the Archduke and his wife Sophie lay dead. Although Princip lived in Bosnia, he was of Serbian heritage. The blame for the Archduke's death would soon be pinned on Serbia.

TESTING OF ALLIANCES

To test the strength of the house of cards, Kaiser Wilhelm demanded that the Austo-Hungarian empire invade Serbia to seek retribution for the Archduke's assassination. After back and forth diplomatic discussions, Serbia finally agreed to investigate the events surrounding the assassination, however, it did not wish for the Austo-Hungarians to be involved in the investigation. As diplomatic discussions grew more intense, Serbia informed Russia that military help might be required. On July 28, 1914, one month after the assassination of the Archduke, the Austro-Hungarian empire declared war against Serbia.

The various alliances that had been agreed to in 1908 swung into action. Germany quickly stepped in with an offer of support to the Austro-Hungarian armies. Russia, in turn, came to Serbia's defense. This brought France to the aid of Russia. Kaiser Wilhelm then made his move. On August 1, 1914, Germany declared war on Russia. Two days later, on August 3, 1914, Germany declared war against France. France reacted with a declaration of war against Germany. Germany then invaded Luxembourg and Belgium.

German boots on the ground in Belgium triggered a response from Britain. In the 1839 *Treaty of London*, Britain had agreed to support Belgian independence. On August 4, 1914, Britain declared war against Germany mainly in an effort to support Belgium but also to prevent France from falling into German hands. Kaiser Wilhelm's goal of making Germany a leading world power was now in play. The European continent was at war. This war would come to be called World War I; the Great War.

THE BATTLE RAGES

World War 1 saw the introduction of "technology" onto the battlefield. For the first time in the history of warfare, aircraft were used to gather reconnaissance data on enemy soldiers. Tanks, machine guns, and poisonous gas were then used to unleash devastating attacks on enemy positions. In the opening month of the conflict, some 750,000 soldiers were killed.

Any notion that this multi-faceted conflict would be short-lived was soon dispelled. By 1916, the conflict was still raging; millions of soldiers and civilians had been wounded and millions more killed. As the end of 1916 loomed, Britain and France had a decision to make: keep fighting and hope for a victory over Germany, or admit a stalemate and negotiate peace. The event that brought them to this decision point was the *Battle of the Somme*. At the height of this battle, British and French troops had managed to advance only 10 kms into German-held territory. The cost of this minor advance was severe. Over 300,000 soldiers from all sides lay dead; over one million soldiers from all sides lay injured.

In Britain, Liberal Prime Minister Herbert Asquith had proven himself inept at managing Britain's war efforts and was forced to resign. David Lloyd George, former Secretary of State for War, replaced him. In France, in response to mounting battlefield casualties, Prime Minister Joseph Caillaux was forced from office and replaced by Georges Clemenceau. Both Clemenceau and Lloyd George had a decision to make: negotiate a peace settlement with Germany or press ahead. Both men decided to press ahead in hopes of defeating Germany.

In Germany, Field Marshall Paul von Hindenburg and Supreme Commander Erich Ludendorff were popular within the German

Reichstag (parliament) and also with Kaiser Wilhelm. They held firm to the idea that Germany could win and should continue fighting. This dogged pursuit would see the conflict drag on for two more painful years.

Eventually America entered the war with a self-serving interest of protecting its global commercial shipping interests from attack by German vessels. Bringing an end to the mounting loss of life and destruction of property in Europe was far down on America's list of priorities. On April 2, 1917, at the urging of President Woodrow Wilson, the U.S. Congress formally declared war on Germany. The U.S. wasted little time in making its presence felt; a series of loans were extended to Britain and France to ensure a steady stream of munitions and supplies to bring about German defeat.

RUSSIA FALTERS

In 1914, Russia had entered the war with millions of troops. But the troops were poorly supplied and the death toll steadily mounted. In 1916, Tsar Nicholas II (House of Romanov) personally took command of the Russian war effort away from the bureaucracy, but the devastation and death toll continued to mount under his leadership. It is estimated that Russia's killed and missing men totaled nearly five million. This staggering death toll left Russian factories idle, farm fields untended, and both food and supplies for the troops in a deficit.

In February 1917, violent demonstrations gripped the streets of Saint Petersburg. People had had enough of the war effort, the idled factories, and the food shortages. Members of the Duma (parliament) defied the Tsar and created a provisional government. Recognizing that his leadership had failed, on March 2, 1917, the Tsar abdicated the throne. His younger brother, Grand Duke Michael Alexandrovich, refused to assume the throne. With that refusal, imperial rule in Russia came to an end. Chaos and governance breakdown followed.

The far-left Bolshevik movement (a faction of the Marxist Russian Social Democratic Labour Party) inspired by the likes of Leon Trotsky and Vladimir Lenin soon gained the support of the people. The Bolshevik movement promised a cessation of the war with Germany, and an end to food shortages.

What Lenin and the Bolsheviks really wanted was absolute power. They began agitating for a military uprising. Workers and soldiers alike responded. By the end of October 1917 (the October Revolution), the House of Romanov was no more. Russia was in the hands of Vladimir Lenin and the Bolsheviks. The country began a descent into a new chapter of civil war and upheaval.

BREST LITOVSK TREATY

Following the October Bolshevik Revolution, Vladimir Lenin appointed a team of negotiators to enter into a deal to take Russia out of the war. By January 1918, the *Brest Litovsk Treaty* had been agreed to. Under this costly agreement, Russia ceded control of Poland, Belarus, Lithuania, Latvia, and Estonia back to Germany and the Austro-Hungarian empire. Large parts of the Caucasus region were ceded back to the Ottoman empire. Russia also agreed to recognize the independence of Finland and to halt its aggression towards Ukraine. These territorial losses and concessions cost Russia half of its previous industrial capacity, most of its coalfields, and a significant portion of its railway network.

GERMANY WEARS OUT

Eight months after the *Brest Litovsk Treaty* was signed, Germany hit a mental tipping point. In August 1918, the British 4th Army made a series of successful advances which deeply affected the attitude of the German military hierarchy. After realizing losses of some 30,000 men on August 8th alone, German Supreme Commander Ludendorff said, "August 8 was a black day for the German Army in the history of the war.…It put the decline of our fighting power beyond all doubt.…The war must be ended."

By late September 1918, the German war effort was thoroughly exhausted and its military leaders were demoralized. Field Marshall von Hindenburg and Commander Ludendorff met with Kaiser Wilhelm II and urged him to enter into war-ending discussions with Allied Power representatives from Britain, France, and the United States. Commander Ludendorff then agreed to cede military decision-making power back to the politicians in the Reichstag.

THE KAISER ABDICATES

With Ludendorff's decision, members of the Reichstag quickly realized that Germany was in trouble. New political leadership was needed immediately. On October 3, 1918, they voted Chancellor Georg von Hertling out and elected Max von Baden as the new Chancellor.

The new Chancellor immediately started to pressure Kaiser Wilhelm to abdicate. The Kaiser refused. To amp up the pressure on the Kaiser, on November 8, 1918, von Baden issued a bold statement saying: "The Emperor and King has decided to abdicate the throne." The Allied Powers spotted their opportunity and gave Germany a timeframe of 72 hours to agree to a cessation of hostilities.

Upon hearing von Baden's statement and upon hearing of the 72-hour demand, reality set in. Kaiser Wilhelm abdicated the throne on November 10, 1918 and made haste for the neutral safety of the Netherlands. The Social Democrat Party with its majority of seats in the Reichstag then announced that Max von Baden had unilaterally appointed Friedrich Ebert as the next Chancellor of Germany.

ARMISTICE

At 5 a.m. on November 11, 1918, an armistice was agreed upon. Hostilities stopped on the front six hours later at 11 a.m. World War I was over.

Of the near 60 million soldiers who had fought on all sides, over 9 million had been killed. Millions more were injured. Millions of civilians had also been killed or injured. The war that had been initiated four years earlier by a series of unstable alliances falling apart, after the firing of an assassin's bullet in Sarajevo, had exacted a staggering price.

Although not realized at the time, this conflict had sown the seeds for a second global war that would erupt in 1939.

NEGOTIATING PEACE

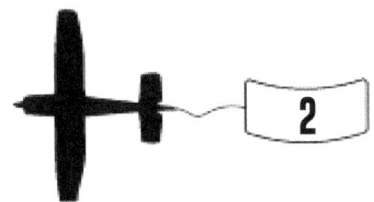

The end of the war set in motion efforts to ensure that such a conflict would never occur again. In January 1919, the Paris Peace Conference was organized. Upon arriving in Paris, delegates from Britain, France, America, Italy, and Japan agreed to form the *Council of Ten*. Delegates from smaller allied nations and neutral nations were not invited to participate in decision making. By March 1919, the Japanese delegates had bowed out and pushed away from the table. Britain, France, America, and Italy now afforded themselves the title *Council of Four.*

The *Council of Four* met several times each day. At each meeting, they debated procedures and studied maps. They also received delegates from a variety of countries seeking to level complaints and make demands. The *Council of Four* soon realized the gravity of the situation across war-torn Europe. Raw material shortages, food shortages, idled factories, shuttered mines, and destroyed railway lines were presenting a recipe for disaster.

The *Council of Four* was also faced with disputes. Greece was annoyed that Serbia had shown up with more delegates. Canadian Prime Minister Robert Borden was annoyed that the British colony of Newfoundland had been asked to attend. More importantly, Russia was conspicuously absent. British delegate Winston Churchill expressed concern that Lenin's ideology could spread beyond Russia's borders.

WILSON'S 14 POINTS

U.S. President Woodrow Wilson was hard at work on a peace document well before the Paris conference. On January 8, 1918, in a speech to Congress, he outlined what he called his *14 Points*. He felt these points should form the framework of any eventual deal to end the hostilities gripping the world.

1. Covenants of peace will be openly arrived at through diplomacy.
2. Countries will enjoy freedom of navigation on the seas outside their territorial waters.
3. All nations consenting to peace will enjoy equality of trade and elimination of economic barriers.
4. Nations consenting to peace will reduce national armaments to the lowest point consistent with domestic safety.
5. A free, open-minded, and absolutely impartial adjustment of all colonial claims will take place.
6. Russian territory will be freed from German troop occupation and Russia will be given cooperation to determine her own political development and national policy.
7. Belgium will be evacuated with no limits placed on her sovereignty.
8. All French territory that has been invaded shall be restored and the wrong done to France by Prussia in 1871 in Alsace-Lorraine region should be righted.

9. A re-adjustment of the frontiers of Italy should be made along recognizable lines of nationality.

10. The peoples of Austria-Hungary should be accorded the freest opportunity of autonomous development.

11. Rumania, Serbia, and Montenegro should be freed from German troop occupation. Serbia should be given free and secure access to the sea. The relations of the Balkan states to one another should be determined by friendly agreement along historically established lines of allegiance and nationality. International guarantees of political and economic independence and territorial integrity of the Balkan states should be entered into.

12. The Turkish portions of the present Ottoman Empire should be assured a secure sovereignty.

13. An independent Polish state should be created and assured free and secure access to the sea.

14. A general association of nations must be formed for the purpose of affording mutual guarantees of political independence and territorial integrity to great and small states alike.

Wilson arrived at the Paris conference certain that his *14 Points* would be incorporated into a formal agreement to create a *League of Nations*. He felt the principle underpinning such a league was that war is a crime against humanity. If all nations agree to join together to prevent war, then war would be unlikely to occur.

Wilson soon realized the naivety of his position when he met pushback from Britain and France on point number 5 which called for an adjustment to colonial claims and holdings. Even though colonial ambitions were at the root of the start of hostilities in 1914, Britain and France were not prepared to relinquish their current or future colonial ambitions.

Further to Wilson's 14th point, the *Council of Four* agreed to set up a 19-man committee to explore the creation of a *League of Nations*. However, behind the scenes, Prime Minister Lloyd George was uninspired by such a league. French Prime Minister Clemenceau privately said he liked the idea, but did not believe in it. Despite the reservations, by April 1919, a draft covenant for the creation of a league had been hammered out.

As the topic of creating a league was being hotly discussed, the *Council of Four* was also dealing with the questions of what a defeated Germany meant for Europe and how much residual power Germany had. The words punishment, payment, and prevention all entered the discussion. Should the Kaiser and his military commanders be tried as war criminals? Should Germany be sent a bill for war damages? What items would the bill contain? How much territory should Germany be forced to concede? The French wanted to deal an economic blow to Germany, but did not want to push the country towards Lenin's ideology. America wanted to restore Germany's industrial capacity but wanted to squelch future military ambitions. Moreover, America wanted Germany to make payments to Britain and France so that they in turn could make good on money borrowed from the U.S. government. Britain owed the U.S. government $4.7 billion. France owed $4 billion.

After months of wrangling, dealing, and thought-provoking debate, the *Council of Four* managed to produce the *Treaty of Versailles* complete with 440 clauses.

THE U.S. SENATE PUSHES BACK

Back in Washington, Woodrow Wilson's pleasure with the progress made in Paris soon turned to dismay. In July 1919, he submitted the treaty to the U.S. Senate for ratification. Massachusetts Republican Henry Cabot Lodge was the Senate majority leader, and the head of the Foreign Relations Committee. Wilson and Lodge made no effort to hide their disdain for one another. So intense was the animosity that Wilson had refused to invite Senator Lodge to the Paris negotiations. This animosity resulted in the Senate rejecting the *Treaty of Versailles*.

Wilson decided to travel across the country to encourage American citizens to pressure their political representatives to adopt the treaty. The travel schedule proved taxing. After giving a speech in Pueblo, Colorado, Wilson collapsed. Back in Washington on October 2, 1919, he suffered a stroke. With his leadership compromised, support for his *14 Points* faded, U.S. approval of the *Treaty of Versailles* was shelved, and his dream of a *League of Nations* died.

GERMANY CONSTRAINED

The *Treaty of Versailles* severely punished Germany. The country was forced to cede to France all control over coal mines in the Saar Basin for 15 years. The Alsace Lorraine region and its potash resources were ceded to France. The Port of Strasbourg and the Port of Kehl were placed under French management. Railways and bridges crossing the Rhine River were placed under French control. Germany was prohibited from establishing fortifications within 50 kms of either side of the Rhine River. Output from German electrical plants was stipulated to remain fixed at November 1918 levels. Germany was forced to recognize the independence of Austria, Czechoslovakia, Poland, the Free City of Danzig, and Egypt. Germany was forced to cede all territory taken from Russia since 1914 and to relinquish all its colonies around the world.

The treaty further forced Germany to reduce its military numbers to fewer than 4,000 officers, seven infantry divisions, and three calvary divisions, employing a combined total of less than 100,000 men. The German air force was required to be demobilized. Weapons, asphyxiating and poisonous gases, and war materials (including 5,000 pieces of artillery, 25,000 machine guns, 1,700 aircraft, 5,000 locomotives, and 150,000 railroad cars) were to be relinquished to the *Council of Four* nations. Furthermore, Germany was restricted to six battleships, six cruisers, 12 destroyers, and 12 torpedo boats. Submarines would be prohibited. All shipbuilding in progress would be halted and dismantled.

Prisoners of war were to be repatriated. All persons who had committed war crimes were to be handed over to the *Council of Four*. A tribunal would be created to try Kaiser Wilhelm for his role in starting the war.

Of all the parts of the treaty, Articles 231 and 232 caused the most angst to Germany. These articles stated that Germany would accept guilt and financial responsibility for losses and damage suffered by all nations as a result of the war. These articles also stated that by May of 1921, a Repatriation Commission would outline a 30-year repayment schedule. As a precursor to what the Commission would decide, Article 235 stated: *in order to enable affected nations to proceed with restoration of their industrial and economic life, pending the full determination of their claims, Germany shall pay in such installments and in such manner (whether in gold, commodities, ships, securities or otherwise) as the Reparation Commission may fix, during 1919, 1920, and the first four months of 1921, the equivalent of 20,000,000,000 gold marks.* In addition to this punishing amount (which was equivalent to U.S. $5 billion), Germany was ordered to deliver every year for the next ten years, seven million tons of coal to France, eight million tons to Belgium, and up to eight million tons to Italy.

In late June 1919, the German parliament was handed the treaty and told it would take effect on January 10, 1920. The Chancellor of Germany at the time, Phillipp Scheidemann, was so disgusted he abruptly resigned from the Reichstag rather than sign the treaty. One of his Ministers, Gustav Bauer, took over the role of Chancellor. Bauer, however, realized he had no room to bargain. He either had to sign the treaty or face invasion and occupation by Britain and France. Germany was now with its back to the wall.

WHY SO HARSH?

Why were the terms of the *Treaty of Versailles* so harsh? The answer is a political-economic one with an aristocratic sub-plot.

A key component of British society is the aristocracy – people of title. The aristocracy is tightly related to the political class who dominate the House of Commons, the House of Lords, and the policies that are created therein. Aristocratic families had no idea that the war would be so severe. Allowing their sons to enlist was seen as the proper thing to do. However, in light of the destruction and loss of life caused by the war, the British aristocracy was determined to never wage war again.

> ... FOR NOT EVEN IN THE GREAT REBELLION AGAINST CHARLES I DID THE NOBILITY LOSE SO MANY OF ITS MEMBERS AS THE LIST OF CASUALTIES OF THE PRESENT WAR DISPLAYS. IN THE FIRST SIXTEEN MONTHS OF OPERATIONS, NO LESS THAN EIGHT HUNDRED MEN OF TITLE WERE KILLED IN ACTION, OR DIED OF THEIR WOUNDS...
>
> – Vanity Fair Magazine, 1916

In addition to the loss of many young aristocratic men, Britain incurred over 700,000 military deaths and double that number of injured soldiers. The steep loss of young life and the staggering number of injured would place a damper on the British economy for several generations to come.

In addition to the human toll, Britain's war debts had translated into inflation, which in turn had stoked union activism. In the interest of political optics, Prime Minister Lloyd George needed to be seen firmly pinning the blame for all of Britain's losses on Germany.

The situation in France was similar. An estimated 10,000 people of noble lineage served in the war effort and nearly 20% of them died. This loss hastened the demographic decline of the noble class and dimmed the future of French elitism.

Moreover, in France, some 712,000 buildings and 20,000 industrial sites had been destroyed or damaged; 2.5 million hectares of farm land had been devastated; 2,000 kilometers of canals had been bombed, 2,000 bridges had been ruined; 62,000 kilometers of roads had been badly damaged, and more than 5,000 kilometers of railroads had been obliterated. France wanted payment for the damage and was not prepared to go easy on the belligerent Germany that had caused the damage. Therefore, during the drafting of the treaty, France maintained a hard, unwavering stance.

Britain's stance did, however, soften slightly. As terms of the treaty were being finalized, Prime Minister Lloyd George wrote a memo to his circle of advisors titled *Some Considerations for the Peace Conference Before They Finally Draft Their Terms*. This document dated March 25, 1919 is often referred to as the *Fontainebleau Memorandum*. One excerpt contains a warning that, although not known at the time, would soon enough come true: *You may strip Germany of her colonies, reduce her armaments to a mere police force, and her navy to that of a*

5th rate power but if she feels she has been unjustly treated in the Peace of 1919, she will find means of extracting retribution from her conquerors.

SETTING THE STAGE

In November 1919, German President von Hindenburg was still in denial over what had happened to Germany. In a speech to the Reichstag, he is on record as saying, "In spite of the superiority of the enemy in men and material, we could have brought the struggle to a favorable issue. Instead, divergent Party interests began to manifest themselves with us. These circumstances soon led to a disintegration of our will to conquer. The German army was stabbed in the back."

Commander Ludendorff – who had receded to the political sidelines – was also in denial. He began voicing sentiment that the State had to control society so that such a defeat never happened again. He stressed that only a dictatorship could do this. Meanwhile, in Vienna, Austria, a thirty-year old starving artist grew increasingly more angered as he followed the news of the *Treaty of Versailles* taking shape. His name was Adolf Hitler and he was becoming enamoured with the sentiment of Ludendorff.

The stage was being set for eventual German retribution. The seeds had been sown for the next major conflict. A conflict that would have implications across western Canada including the small farming town of Mossbank, Saskatchewan.

ADOLF HITLER

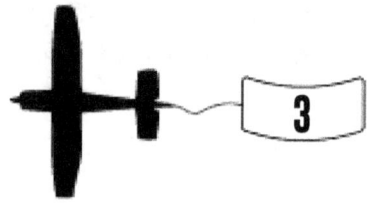

Adolf Hitler's father, Alois, started out as a shoemaker in the Austrian village of Spital. Boredom soon had him moving to Vienna to take up work with the Austrian Customs Service. His first marriage lasted 16 years and produced no children. His next marriage was to a young hotel cook, Franziska Matzelberger, who gave him a son, also called Alois, and a daughter Angela. When Franziska died in 1885, Alois married a third time – to his second cousin, Klara Pöelzl. Their first two children died in infancy. Another son, born in 1894, died at the age of six.

Alois Hitler retired from his customs inspection job in 1895. In the years immediately afterward, the family moved numerous times. Adolf was born on April 20, 1889 in Braunau am Inn, a small town in southern Germany near the border with Austria. The final child born to Alois and Klara was a daughter, Paula. Alois had a cold, silent personality and was reportedly very hard on young Adolf. Klara, on the other hand, was reportedly warm, loving, and kindhearted.

LAZY AND REBELLIOUS

By the time Adolf was in grade five, the family was living in Linz, Austria. From an early age, Adolf expressed interest in becoming an artist. Alois strictly forbade him to do so, feeling that the only path for Adolf would be the civil service and possibly a job with the Customs Service. This imposition had a deleterious effect on Adolf's attitude. He became lazy and at times rebellious. His marks in school suffered. Unable to motivate him, school authorities transferred Adolf to a new school in nearby Steyr, Austria. However, the laziness and bad attitude continued as did the poor marks. Shortly after the transfer, his father died suddenly of a stroke. His mother then died shortly afterwards of complications related to pneumonia. At the age of 13, Adolf dropped out of school.

He was now lazy, rebellious, orphaned, and without direction. However, the strong anti-Semitic cultural currents flowing through Austrian society at the time soon gave him direction. He decided he did not like Austria, Marxism, the Social Democrat Party, labour unions, the Austrian press, or Jews.

REJECTION

Adolf's childhood goal of becoming an artist was sincere. He had artistic talent; in particular, he was very skilled at sketching and painting buildings. He tried on two occasions to gain acceptance into the Vienna Art Academy. Perhaps because of his failure to graduate from school, perhaps because of his general demeanour, he was rejected both times. However, the Academy did suggest to him that he would be a good fit for its architecture program. However, to gain admission to the program, he would have to complete his high school diploma and then undertake several prerequisite studies. He decided that he was unwilling to fulfill these requirements.

Rejection by the Academy hardened his demeanour towards the world. However, he needed to find his way in the world. He needed to eat; to make a living. He started earning small sums of spending money by painting postcards and selling them on the street. He also did menial jobs such as shoveling snow and carrying luggage at the railway station. The small amounts he earned allowed him to stay in men's shelters in Vienna and eat in soup kitchens.

One day, he was approached and asked to join a union. He flatly refused the offer. He felt that unions were targeting the weak, unskilled labourers in Vienna. He felt unions were an extension of the Social Democratic political movement, popular in Austria at the time. Moreover, even though the population of Vienna was only 10% Jewish, he felt Jews were at the heart and soul of the Social Democratic movement. This was a pivotal moment in Adolf's life.

He became fascinated with the views of radical politicians Georg Ritter von Schönerer and Karl Lueger. Influenced by the ideas of these radicals, Adolf Hitler became an avowed anti-Semite. He came to the conclusion that Jews were behind not only Social Democracy, but also the press, the arts, literature, theatre, and even prostitution. He developed a vision of the future which focused on an ethnically pure German national state that would expand by conquering Russia. He further felt that the Marxist socialist movement in Russia was rooted in Jewish doctrine and must be stamped out in a life or death fight.

I BELIEVE I AM ACTING IN ACCORDANCE WITH THE WILL OF THE ALMIGHTY CREATOR: BY DEFENDING MYSELF AGAINST THE JEWS, I AM FIGHTING FOR THE WORK OF THE LORD.

– Adolf Hitler, *Mein Kampf*

AN EXCELLENT SOLDIER

Unable to gain acceptance into the Art Academy, unable to find meaningful employment, unable to reconcile himself with Austrian society, and facing the prospect of being conscripted into the Austrian army, in 1913 Adolf moved to Munich, Germany where he voluntarily joined the Bavarian Infantry Regiment. He felt compelled to support the leader of Germany – Kaiser Wilhelm.

> SO, ALL THE SACRIFICES AND PRIVATIONS HAD BEEN IN VAIN; IN VAIN THE HOURS IN WHICH, WITH MORTAL FEAR CLUTCHING AT OUR HEARTS, WE NEVERTHELESS DID OUR DUTY. DID ALL THIS HAPPEN SO THAT A GANG OF WRETCHED CRIMINALS COULD LAY HANDS ON THE FATHERLAND?
>
> – Adolf Hitler, *Diary*, November 1918

> I WAS REPELLED BY THE CONGLOMERATION OF RACES WHICH VIENNA SHOWED ME, REPELLED BY THIS WHOLE MIXTURE OF CZECHS, POLES, HUNGARIANS, RUTHENIANS, SERBS, AND CROATS, AND EVERYWHERE THE ETERNAL MUSHROOM OF HUMANITY – JEWS AND MORE JEWS. TO ME THIS CITY SEEMED THE EMBODIMENT OF RACIAL DESECRATION.
>
> – Adolf Hitler, *Mein Kampf*

When conflict erupted in 1914, the Bavarian Infantry Regiment sent him to the front lines. He served a total of four years in the military; he was reportedly a very good soldier, was wounded twice in mustard gas attacks, and once by shrapnel to his leg. For perhaps the first time in his life, he felt a sense of belonging. His soldiering skills drew the attention of his superiors who offered him promotions. He refused these promotions so he could stay with the Infantry Regiment and enjoy a sense of belonging. In 1918, as the war was nearing an end, he was awarded the Iron Cross First Class for his contribution to the war effort.

HATRED

His rebellious attitude resurfaced with the defeat of Germany and the abdication of Kaiser Wilhelm. Adolf turned his attention to politics, which gave him an outlet for his rebellious energies. He felt that Jewish financiers were responsible for the war and were behind German Field Marshall von Hindenberg being forced to surrender to the Allied Powers.

With the Kaiser gone, Friedrich Ebert, the leader of the left-wing Social Democratic Party, was tasked with forming a government. In late 1918, Ebert and his Party members started drafting a new German Constitution and by late summer 1919, had it finalized. In the spring of 1920, the first elections in the new Republic of Germany were held; Ebert's Party won a majority of seats and formed government. Ebert was then elected as President of the new Republic of Germany.

Ebert's election to President incensed Adolf Hitler. He held in contempt anyone who had not supported the Kaiser in the final months of the war. He felt the Kaiser had been stabbed in the back by left-wing, Marxist Jews.

He felt the Social Democratic party was focused too intently on international finance and stock market valuation. His hatred was further fueled by the writings of German engineer and construction company owner Gottfried Feder who harbored ill feelings towards bankers in light of the *Treaty of Versailles*. Feder expressed his ill feelings in *Brechung der Zinsknechtschaft* - a manifesto that argued bank interest on its debt was hurting Germany's economy. The manifesto further argued that banks should be nationalized and interest on debt abolished.

GERMAN WORKER'S PARTY

Adolf's rebellious attitude drew the attention of the far-right *German Worker's Party*, a movement started by Feder and right-wing political agitator, Anton Drexler. When Drexler asked Adolf to join the movement, the invitation was gladly accepted. Adolf Hitler became member #7 in the fledgling movement.

Exposure to the Party philosophy aligned with Hitler's anti-Semitic views. He came to feel that the pure German race (the Aryan race) was at the root of human creation and at the root of science and technology. He felt that the Aryan race represented the mightiest counterbalance to the Jews.

The fledgling Party quickly gathered momentum. By early 1920, the Party had raised enough money from selling memberships that it could now afford to print pamphlets and posters to better promote itself. One of the pamphlets that Drexler designed was titled *My Political Awakening*. After reading the pamphlet which was filled with anti-Semitic, anti-capitalist ideas, Adolf felt that same sense of belonging he had felt in the Infantry. The German Worker's Party was for him.

Hitler's decision to become more deeply involved in politics soon revealed that he had a skillset that he had previously been unaware of; he found that he had the confidence to speak in front of large gatherings of people.

BOMBS AWAY!

IN THIS FIRST MEETING, I HAD BEEN GRANTED 20
MINUTES OF SPEAKING TIME. I SPOKE FOR 30 MINUTES
AND WHAT BEFORE I HAD SIMPLY FELT WITHIN ME
WAS NOW PROVED BY REALITY: I COULD SPEAK!

– Adolf Hitler, *Mein Kampf*

Drexler soon had Adolf travelling throughout Germany promoting the Party platform. Adolf spoke of the humiliation of Germany at the hands of the Allied Powers. He spoke of the need for Germany to expand beyond its current borders that had been redrawn as part of the *Treaty of Versailles*. He spoke of the need to kill the *Treaty of Versailles* which he labeled a shame, a disgrace, and an effort to pillage the German people. He spoke of the need to create a strong central power in Germany and to unify all German speaking people into a greater Germany. He spoke out against Communism. He spoke out against the wealthy merchant class and against capitalism. He spoke in favor of corporate profit sharing with the State. He demanded the death penalty for traitors and profiteers. He also began openly expressing harsh anti-Semitic views. Adolf Hitler's speech-making skills soon positioned him as a rising star in the *German Worker's Party*.

He next convinced Drexler that the Party needed an emblem. With input from Munich-based goldsmith, Otto Gahr, he designed a flag with a red background and white disc in the middle. Inside the disc was black swastika (the hooked cross, or *hakenkreuz*). He viewed the red as representing socialist ideals, white the idea of nationalism, and the swastika the struggle of victory of Aryan man.

REBRANDING

In July 1921, at a Party meeting, members overwhelmingly voted Adolf Hitler to the position of Party leader. Members then passed resolutions granting him almost complete power in running the Party.

With this unbridled grip on power, he immediately took steps to rebrand the Party as the *Nationalsozialistische Deutsche Arbeiterpartei* (NSDAP). This lengthy name was soon shortened to the *Nazi Party*.

LIKE-MINDED FRIENDS

Adolf Hitler was not alone at the helm of the NSDAP. He had become acquainted with Rudolph Hess, a war veteran with strong anti-Semitic views and wild-eyed ideas. He also gravitated towards Alfred Rosenberg, a former Russian intellectual who had renounced Russia and joined the German Army during the invasion of Russia. Rosenberg held a diploma in architecture studies from the University of Moscow; this may have been the basis for the mutual attraction. Hermann Göring had been the Commander of the famous Richthofen fighter squadron in World War I; he was charmed by Hitler's personality and soon became a faithful disciple. The list of faithful went on to include a long roster of murderers, thugs, thieves, and violent social misfits.

BEER HALL RALLIES

Hitler's efforts contributed to the NSDAP becoming popular enough that it started holding rallies in large beer halls across Germany. At one meeting in 1921 at the Zirkus Krone Hall in Munich, over 6,000 people were in attendance to hear Party leaders speak on the theme of "Future or Ruin." At a similar event several months later at the Munich Hofbrauhaus, thousands listened to speeches that equated the stock market with Jews; to sentiment that described the sweating of the German working class under the yoke of Jewish world finance; and to the idea that the Armistice of 1918 was the start of a movement to steer Germany into total submission.

Despite the apparent popularity of the Party rallies, Hitler was nervous for his safety and that of key Party members. To provide for security, Hitler encouraged the more militant Party faithful to join a group called the SA (*Sturmabteilung*). Members of the SA were easily recognizable with their mandated brown shirts and brown ties. Their mission was to provide security at Party meetings, march in street rallies, and physically attack people who were opposed to the Party.

Under Hitler's absolute control, the central tenet of the Party quickly evolved into one of anti-Semitism. The seeds planted by the *Treaty of Versailles* were starting to germinate.

PAYMENT AND PUNISHMENT

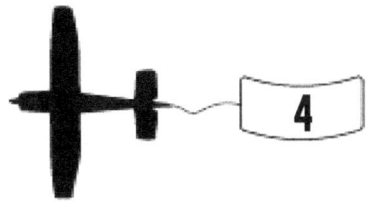

Article 233 of the *Treaty of Versailles* called for Germany's repayment schedule to be defined by May 1921. By January 1921, members of the Reparation Commission (Belgium, France, Italy, Japan, Serbia, Croatia, Britain, and the U.S.) still had not reached consensus on a definitive payment schedule. With the deadline looming, France, Britain, and the U.S. took charge and presented Germany with the *London Ultimatum* which called for Germany to assume responsibility for repayment of the total estimated wartime damages of 132 billion gold marks. (Note - prior to the start of the war, Germany had been on the gold standard and 2,790 marks of paper currency were deemed equivalent to 1 kg of gold). The sum of 132 billion gold marks was a staggering figure - the equivalent of just over US$1 trillion in today's money. Germany was given a handful of days (until May 4, 1921) to accept the ultimatum.

The repayment scheme was anything but straightforward. The 132 billion gold mark total was divided into several components: Category A bonds worth 12 billion gold marks carrying an interest rate of 5% compounded over 30 years, Category B bonds worth 38 billion gold marks carrying an interest rate of 5% compounded over 30 years, and Category C bonds worth 82 billion gold marks carrying no interest. The creators of the *London Ultimatum* were aware that the German Reichsbank could use its printing press to create enough currency to meet the payment schedules. To prevent the printing press from being exclusively used to pay, the *London Ultimatum* stated that Germany would have to annually remit an amount of money equivalent to 26% of its annual exports (approximately 3 billion gold marks). Once the export remittances totaled 50 billion gold marks, the Category A and B bonds would be deemed repaid and Germany would then be left with having to repay only 89 billion gold marks of interest-free Category C bonds.

Realizing the magnitude of this 132 billion gold mark financial undertaking, Chancellor Constantin Fehrenbach resigned. Fehrenbach was succeeded by Joseph Wirth who decided he would do as much as possible to follow the *London Ultimatum* while at the same time keeping the German economy afloat.

PRINTING MONEY

Chancellor Wirth decided he would use the printing press to a certain extent. He would have the Reichsbank print only as much money as would be needed to keep the economy functioning so as to generate exports to pay for the Category A and B bonds. Wirth hoped that Britain, France, and the U.S. would recognize Germany's good faith approach at making the scheduled payments and offer some concessions in appreciation. His strategy did not work; no concessions were made by either country. The French government under Prime

Minister Poincare definitely showed no mercy and went so far as to argue that the French government should take back some territory from Germany as a further reparation penalty.

Faced with this lack of sympathy, Wirth resigned and was succeeded by Wilhelm Cuno who was confident that the German economy would become strong enough that the A and B bonds could be quickly paid off. What Cuno failed to take into account was that the money being printed to keep the economy functioning was fueling inflation and undermining confidence in the German currency. Capital started fleeing the country creating additional downward pressure on the German currency. To keep the economy running, Cuno had to print more money, which further fueled inflation.

POINCARE GETS TOUGH

Currency confidence concerns and inflation worries aside, with Germany now making payments, British Prime Minister David Lloyd George started working with Italian officials to organize the *Genoa Conference for Economic and Financial Reconstruction*. The event would be held in Genoa from April 10 to May 19, 1922. The hope was that the conference would pave the way for a reopening of trade between Britain, France, Germany, and Russia. However, the French government proved difficult, agreeing to attend on the condition that no changes would be made to the *Treaty of Versailles*. France still desperately wanted to deal a crushing blow to Germany. (At the root of this desire was the Bolshevik Revolution. Following the revolution, Vladimir Lenin ordered a default on all Russian debts owed to foreign nations. This default destroyed the investment savings of nearly one million French people. In a twisted bit of logic, France now wanted to extract as much money as possible from Germany to help restore the losses exacted by Russia on these French investors.)

Despite the hard edge being displayed by France, Italian Prime Minister Luigi Facta expressed hope that by the end of the conference there would no longer be "friends and enemies, victors and vanquished." The British delegation turned its focus to dialogue aimed at finding common ground with France to calm the aggressive French sentiment towards Germany.

RAPALLO TREATY

The hard edge being displayed by the French delegation led to an unusual turn of events in Genoa. During sideline discussions between German and Russian delegates, the *Rapallo Treaty* was quickly agreed to. This Treaty ruled out Germany having to make reparation payments to Russia, restored diplomatic relations between the two countries, opened the way for German companies to resume work in the Russian oilfields, and set the stage for a limited sharing of military technology.

To say that Britain and France were furious at this development is an understatement. Germany had completely gone around the two nations and cozied up to Russia. However, while David Lloyd George was infuriated, he was not surprised. He had long been warning France that if Germany was treated too harshly, the Germans would pivot towards the Russians.

RUHR VALLEY OCCUPATION

French Prime Minister Raymond Poincare made it clear that, going forward, France would deal unilaterally with Germany. No more negotiating. No more talk of possible concessions. France was taking a hard stand and that was all there was to it. Poincare then instructed his military commander Marshall Foch to draw up a plan for French troops to occupy the coal-rich Ruhr Valley area of Germany in the event that Germany defaulted on any of its repayments.

Britain tried in vain to reason with France. During the first week of January 1923, Germany defaulted on one of its scheduled reparation payments. With that, France took its promised unilateral action. On January 11, French and Belgian troops marched into the coal-mining Ruhr valley region near Essen, Germany and took control of the coal mines.

Unexpectedly, the effort backfired. Coal mine owners, government officials – even hotel and restaurant owners – all refused to co-operate with the troops. Railroad and river navigation officials halted all rail and boat traffic. French authorities intensified the situation by confiscating coal mine owner's funds from banks, and by fining, imprisoning, and even deporting some local government officials, mine owners, mine superintendents, customs officials, and railway employees. They even forcibly closed hotels, restaurants, and shops that had refused to cooperate with troops. As many coal mines shut down, German steel mills were forced to stop production; industrial activity across Germany slowed.

Adolf Hitler was watching these events transpire. On January 18, 1923, he went on the defensive. At a small rally at Munich's Café Neumayr he asked those in attendance to fantasize with him about a mass hanging of French occupying troops.

"WE KNOW VERY WELL THAT IF THE OTHERS TAKE THE HELM, OUR HEADS WILL ROLL IN THE SAND. BUT THIS ONE THING I CRY: IF WE GET TO THE HELM, THEN WOE TO THE OTHERS. THEIR HEADS WILL BE THE ONES TO ROLL! ONE OF US WILL BE LEFT ON THE GROUND, THE WHEEL WILL ROLL OVER ONE OF US!"

– Adolf Hitler

He made it clear what he would do if his Party rose to political dominance. His anger and aggression were now on full display. Germany was about to implode, or so it felt.

FAILED INSURRECTION

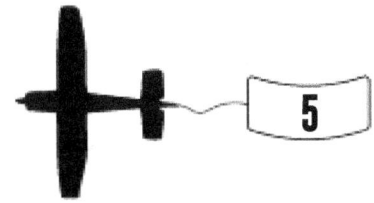

By late 1922, the NSDAP was riding an unprecedented wave of popularity. To celebrate this popularity, a Party convention was planned for early January 1923. To stir up emotion ahead of this event, Adolf Hitler delivered speeches referring to Jews as the deadly enemy of the German race.

Having absolute power over the NSDAP swelled Adolf Hitler's ego. In early 1923, German newspaper *Volkischer Beobachter* compared him to the likes of Otto von Bismarck and Friedrich the Great. The paper went on to say that once Hitler had destroyed the current political establishment, his leadership would make Germany great again.

"Making Germany great again" was a theme that further inflated his ego. He began hinting strongly that the members of the Reichstag should make him the Chancellor of Germany.

THE NEW FLAG

One of the main goals of the planned NSDAP Convention was to proudly display the new flag of the NSDAP that had been designed in 1921. In an effort to avoid a huge spectacle, the German Interior Ministry ordered the Munich police to outlaw outdoor events, marches, parades, and flag raisings. The Bavarian government went further and declared a State of Emergency. Hitler and influential Party member Ernst Rohm met with authorities and promised to keep events at the conference under control. Authorities relented and the conference went ahead as planned. On January 28, 1923, the new Nazi flag was hoisted outside the conference venue.

> "NO ONE OF THAT RACE, WHO ARE OUR ENEMIES, WHO HAVE LED US INTO GREAT MISERY, NO JEW, SHALL EVER TOUCH THIS FLAG. IT SHALL FLY AHEAD OF US IN OUR TRIUMPHANT MARCH ACROSS ALL GERMANY, AND BE THE PROTOTYPE FOR THE NEW GERMAN NATIONAL FLAG."
>
> – Adolf Hitler (January 1923)

At the business and policy session of the conference, members voted in favor of Adolf Hitler remaining as Party leader and gave him permission to choose his fellow leaders. The Party members also voted in favor of a resolution that declared the *Treaty of Versailles* null and void. The resolution further called for ruthless suppression of all traitors to the Fatherland, freedom of all German prisoners of war, and arrest of the politicians who failed to support Kaiser Wilhelm.

The Party was not alone in its stance. Other right-wing organizations such as League Bavaria and the Oberland League had similar ideals. But none of these other right-wing groups had a leader with the charisma and speaking talents of Adolf Hitler.

A STRONGER SA

However inflated his ego was, Adolf Hitler was also a cautious man. He and his NSDAP (Nazi Party) faithful were fearful that the economically damaged German economy would lead to an increase in Communist sentiment among voters. He was also aware of the growing popularity of private militia groups in Germany who were intent on stamping out Communist sentiment in Germany as a way of making Germany great again. These groups soon began appearing at Nazi Party rallies. However, Hitler had no positional authority over these break-away groups. He could not have them competing with him on the theme of making Germany great again. To prevent these groups from gaining further popularity and possibly turning against the Nazi Party, he decided to give the SA (*Sturmabteilung*) a broader mandate to protect the Party and its members. In early 1923, Hitler named Hermann Göring as head of the SA. This marked the beginning of Göring's rise to fame in the Nazi Party.

BEER HALL INSURRECTION

The SA soon turned their broadened mandate into a program of violence against Jews. This program was concentrated in the Ruhr region where the SA made the argument that the Jews were in collaboration with the French and Belgian occupying troops. *Volkischer Beobachter* editor Hermann Esser began calling for a mass murder of Jews in the area. His logic was that if 50,000 Jews were murdered, foreign investment capital would be motivated to return to Germany. This logic attracted the attention of Hitler who began calling for a May 1 (May Day) Jewish massacre. At the last minute, army leader Otto von Lossow withdrew his support of a May Day event and catastrophe was averted. Lossow's decision further hardened Adolf Hitler. He realized that if the agenda of the Nazi Party was going to advance, he would have to make decisions unilaterally. No more relying on others.

Having seen Benito Mussolini use the power of the spoken word to excite people at a large rally in Rome in 1922, Adolf Hitler reasoned that he could orchestrate something similar in Germany. In early November 1923, a crowd of nearly 3,000 gathered in Munich at the Bürgerbräukeller beer hall to hear a speech by far-right politician Gustav Ritter von Kahr. Among those assembled was Adolf Hitler. As von Kahr spoke inside, hundreds of members of Göring's SA surrounded the venue outside.

Towards the end of von Kahr's speech, Adolf Hitler made a sudden rush for the stage, climbed onto a chair, fired his pistol at the ceiling and yelled, "National revolution is underway!" He told the crowd that hundreds of armed SA were outside the hall and that nobody could leave the premises. His antics quickly degraded into confusion. He left the building and ordered the SA to march with him through the streets of Munich.

The marchers soon encountered law enforcement officials. In the ensuing clash, four police officers and 16 Nazi Party followers were killed. Several days later, Adolf Hitler was arrested and charged with high treason. When his trial began in early 1924, he decided to use the courtroom to promote his far-right ideas. Over the course of the 24-day trial, he gave several long-winded speeches in the courtroom in his own defense. He also directed several terse outbursts at the judges.

"FOR IT IS NOT YOU, GENTLEMEN WHO PASS JUDGEMENT ON US. THAT JUDGEMENT IS SPOKEN BY THE ETERNAL COURT OF HISTORY. YOU MAY PRONOUNCE US GUILTY A THOUSAND TIMES OVER, BUT THE GODDESS OF THE ETERNAL COURT OF HISTORY WILL SMILE AND TEAR TO

TATTERS THE BRIEF OF THE STATE PROSECUTOR AND THE
SENTENCE OF THIS COURT. FOR SHE ACQUITS US."

– Adolf Hitler

The court officials did nothing to stop him. Not only had the German government been pressuring the judiciary to let Adolf Hitler continue his courtroom antics so as to get the trial over with quickly, the courtroom judges were already of a right-of-center persuasion and were only too happy to tolerate his antics.

In one of his final courtroom orations, Hitler blamed Germany's economic decline on Jews and Communists. He made it clear his goal was to restore Germany to its former glory. On April 1, 1924, he was found guilty of high treason.

His sentence was light; five years in prison with eligibility for parole after nine months. While he was arguably guilty as charged, his outbursts and orations in court had made him, in the eyes of many Germans, a patriot and a hero.

During his confinement in Landsberg prison, he spent his days writing. The result was *Mein Kampf* – his personal story and manifesto. The text made clear his bitter resentment over Germany's defeat. His words left no doubt that that in his mind Jews were plotting to take control of Germany. He expanded on his ideas of making a new state based on race superiority to be ruled by an absolute leader.

Once in print and widely available, *Mein Kampf* - all 782 pages of it - was fanatically embraced by millions of Germans. Had more foreign leaders read it, perhaps Adolf Hitler could have been diverted off his trajectory.

HYPERINFLATION

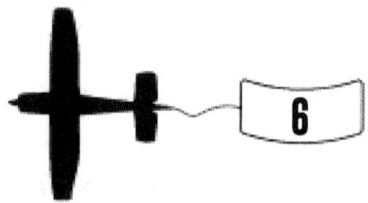

With the coal-mining Ruhr regions under occupation by French and Belgian troops, workers in the mines began demonstrating passive resistance by slowing their pace of work. French authorities reduced their pay accordingly. The German government decided to initiate a program of reimbursing the workers for lost wages, providing they continued their passive resistance against the occupying troops. To generate the money to make these payments, the Reichsbank resorted to the printing press. Passive resistance also meant a reduction in coal output for domestic use. Further currency was printed so that Germany could purchase coal from other European countries.

The Reichsbank printing presses injected nearly three trillion marks per month of freshly printed paper money into the economy. Inflation surged. In June 1922, 317 marks bought US$1; by December 1922, it took on average 7,589 marks to buy US$1. The Reichsbank was sourcing paper from a reported 30 paper factories because the printing companies contracted to print banknotes were running a reported 1,800 banknote printing presses to produce sufficient currency.

People and businesses began liquidating their marks and converting them to other currencies at a furious pace. This liquidation started the German currency on a trajectory to worthlessness. By May 1923, it took 25,000 marks to buy US$1. By July the exchange rate had risen to an average of 353,400 marks to US$1; by November it took 2.1 trillion German currency units to buy US$1.

Initially, businessmen and landowners with mortgages benefited from the inflation as they repaid loans with marks that were effectively worthless. Farmers benefited from the weak currency as they received steadily more currency units for their produce. However, factory workers who still had jobs to go needed to renegotiate their wages daily. Soon an average German family needed 110,000 marks per week just to survive. As the German mark faltered, pensioners on fixed incomes were financially hard done-by as they had no way to increase their income. Nearly half of all children were under-nourished and only partially clothed. Diphtheria, tuberculosis, measles, and rickets began to spread through the population.

As the run on the currency continued and as government tax revenues dwindled, the Reichsbank resorted to printing even more money, fueling further declines in the currency's purchasing power. It was a spiral to the bottom. Landlords hemmed in by rent control legislation made next to nothing in profit for renting their commercial properties; retail businesses in these commercial buildings were open only sporadically because sourcing merchandise to put on the shelves became difficult.

By late 1923, the currency was worthless. Farmers refused to sell their produce valued in German marks. Factory activity ground to a near halt. Riots and robberies were commonplace in towns and cities across the country. After 264 days, Cuno was ousted as Chancellor. He had failed.

The economic malaise spread hatred and resentment throughout Germany. The sense of unfairness was amplified by knowledge that many elite members of society had transferred their money out of German marks and into U.S. dollars. They had invested in the rising U.S. stock market and had won big. Names like Stinnes, Wolff, Flick, Karstadt, Herzfeld, and Hugenberg came to be known as the "Kings of Inflation." Knowledge that some members of society had profited from the currency demise did not sit well with the average German. People made the illogical leap to suggest that Jews were behind the currency crisis; the flames of anti-Semitism were further fanned.

FRANCE'S AGGRESSION AND BRITAIN'S TEMERITY

The passive resistance effort in the Ruhr Valley was hurting France. Initially, France reasoned that by occupying the region, it could ensure a steady supply of coal for itself while exacting revenge on Germany. Instead, the opposite was happening. As German mine workers displayed passive resistance, coal output dwindled. Nevertheless, the stubborn French Prime Minister, Raymond Poincare, ordered his troops to stay the course.

In August 1923, German President Ebert appointed career bureaucrat Gustav Stresemann as Chancellor. Where Cuno had failed, Stresemann made progress, thanks to Britain reaching the point of complete annoyance with the French attitude. British Prime Minister Stanley Baldwin warned France to ease up on the Ruhr region occupation. He warned that Britain deemed the occupation to be illegal and that if France did not withdraw its troops, Britain would no longer be able to support France in trade or security agreements.

Baldwin then suggested that an international panel of financial experts be assembled to examine the finances of Germany to determine just what Germany could afford to pay in terms of reparations.

French Prime Minister Poincare gambled that if he did not immediately respond to Britain's warnings, the British would back off. His gamble proved astute. Britain did not move to take any follow-up action against France and the French rejection of Baldwin's overtures landed a bruising blow on British influence in European affairs. Poincare and the French government rejoiced in their political victory.

With the German economy crippled, the members of the Reichstag desperately needed a solution. On October 13, 1923, an enabling law was passed which granted Stresemann extraordinary powers to save the German economy.

THE DAWES PLAN

The repayment schedule imposed by the *London Ultimatum* was obviously not working. The Reparation Commission decided it had to take swift action. It struck a committee to explore a solution and appointed Chicago investment banker Charles Dawes to head up the committee. Dawes drafted a plan (the *Dawes Plan*) which Stresemann agreed to. The *Dawes Plan* called for a Germany to make repayments of 1 billion marks per year in years 1-5, and 2.5 billion marks per year after year 5. The full amount of reparation payments would be decided at a later date. As well, France and Belgium would remove their troops from the Ruhr region.

The *Dawes Plan* further called for German economic policy to fall under supervision of Britain, France, and the U.S. The German mark would be replaced by a new currency - the Reichsmark. U.S. finance magnate J.P. Morgan agreed to invest US$200 million to aid in German economic stabilization. This move by Morgan sparked the attention of the U.S. banking sector which suddenly expressed a new willingness to lend to Germany. These loans would finally assist Germany in making its scheduled payments to France and Britain, who in turn would then make repayments on money they had borrowed from the U.S. government during the war.

The *Dawes Plan* promised to be a win-win for all. French Prime Minister Poincare agreed to remove his troops from the Ruhr region. Chancellor Stresemann in turn agreed to end the passive resistance movement.

As the Ruhr area coal mines slowly returned to full production, Stresemann followed the *Dawes Plan* and refinanced the German banking system with the new Reichsmark. Management, labour, and unions were told to adopt a ten-hour workday and, where possible, a two-shift schedule of operations. Many government employees were made redundant and those that remained employed were dealt a 25% wage cut. A slate of new corporate taxes was also levied.

Stresemann's efforts worked. By early 1924, the German financial situation was back in balance. Prices had stabilized; confidence had started to return. However, despite Stresemann's successful efforts, the Reichstag remained divided along Party lines. On November 30, 1923, the German National People's Party, the Social Democratic Party, and the Communist Party acted together on a motion of non-confidence to bring down the government of Stresemann. The motion passed. Stresemann suddenly found himself out. He was succeeded by the Centre Party's Wilhelm Marx.

MORE POWERFUL THAN EVER

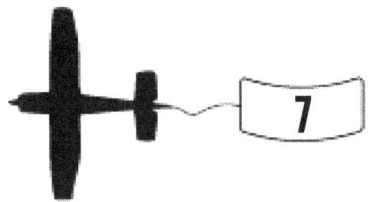

Adolf Hitler watched the *Dawes Plan* unfold from behind bars. When he was paroled in December 1924, after serving nine months of his sentence for high treason, he picked up where he had left off. He promised his followers that their struggle to make Germany strong again would start anew.

A condition of his parole was that he not give public speeches. Not only did the court system feel that this condition would silence him, thanks to Chancellor Stresemann and the *Dawes Plan,* the German economy had been put back on firmer footing. With people feeling confident again, the court believed the Nazi Party would find it more difficult to draw an audience to hear the Party's message.

But what the courts did not realize was that Adolf Hitler was not about to go quietly. He was a man of dogged persistence. Nor could the courts envision the series of events that would soon unfold. President Ebert was ill and in February 1925 he died. His death brought 78-year-old Paul von Hindenberg back into politics. In the March 1925 elections, von Hindenberg was elected President.

In the December 1925 elections, the Nazi Party saw its popularity reduced by half from the previous election. The economy was stable. People were rebuilding their lives. There was little room for the hard-core, right-of-center Nazi philosophy. In the 1928 elections, the numbers further declined. The Nazi Party took only 12 seats and 3% of the vote. The sun was setting on the Nazi Party and on Adolf Hitler. Or was it?

Adolf Hitler decided that if he had restrictions placed on him as part of his parole, he would seek ways of gaining power by legitimate means. He would rebuild the Nazi Party. He was not prepared to go away. He began travelling across the country, meeting with people who were interested in the Nazi platform. His hard work and promotion efforts raised membership numbers from a low of 27,000 in 1925 to 178,000 by 1929. As numbers grew, he reorganized the Party.

He created the *Hitler Jungen* (Hitler Youth) to indoctrinate young people with far-right views. He also created an entity called the *Schutzstaffel* (SS) to protect Party insiders, promote Nazi racial policy, and to root out enemies of the Nazi movement. (The SA was still in existence, but had become splintered during Hitler's nine-month absence in prison. Hitler felt the fractured SA might no longer be loyal to him.)

"INSTEAD OF WORKING TO ACHIEVE POWER BY ARMED COUP, WE SHALL HAVE TO HOLD OUR NOSES AND ENTER THE REICHSTAG AGAINST THE OPPOSITION DEPUTIES. IF OUTVOTING THEM TAKES LONGER THAN OUTSHOOTING THEM, SOONER OR LATER WE SHALL HAVE A MAJORITY AND AFTER THAT – GERMANY."

– Adolf Hitler

To boast of his accomplishments, he returned to the scene of the crime, the Bürgerbräukeller beer hall, where he gave a speech announcing himself as the supreme leader of the Nazi Party. He then set his sights on getting his Party elected to power.

His efforts received an unexpected boost thanks to the U.S. stock market collapse in October 1929 which immediately plunged much of the world, including Germany, into economic depression. Under the *Dawes Plan*, Germany had borrowed sizeable sums of money from U.S. banks to help finance industrial expansion. As the economy slowed, industry ground to a near halt. Germany entered a dark period as millions of factory workers were thrown out of work. Small businesses shut their doors. Banks collapsed. Meanwhile, the interest on Germany's borrowed money kept compounding. Adolf Hitler decided to turn the misery of the German people into his own political advantage.

PERCEPTION MATTERS

Elections were called for September 14, 1930. The Nazi Party ran an aggressive campaign. Adolf Hitler promised he would make Germany strong again. He would put an end to reparation payments. He would cancel the *Versailles Treaty*. He would end political corruption. He would make sure that every German who wanted a job got one.

Voters took notice. After the votes were counted, the Nazi Party had taken 37% of the popular vote (nearly 13 million votes) and had won 230 seats in the Reichstag. The Nazi Party was now the second-largest party in Germany. This surge in popularity was of immediate concern to foreign investors who began to fear that their loans to German businesses might be in peril. In the weeks following the election, 800 million Reichmarks (US$2.8 billion today) in deposit money was removed from German banks.

In politics, perception matters. Of the near 13 million people who voted for the Nazi Party, only a fraction had ever seen Adolf Hitler at rallies. But all had either heard of him or had read about him in the press. The image that people cultivated in their minds of a person who was going to make Germany great again matched what they had heard and read. In many communities, respected businessmen and leaders voiced favorable opinions of the Nazi Party, That was enough to get citizens to cast their votes in favor of the Party. Adolf Hitler also proved himself adept at reading the anger of people who were being impacted by the slowing economy. He voiced simple and easy-to-understand ideas of how to make Germany great again. These ideas, wrapped in slogans and themes, were all people needed to hear as they decided who they would vote for.

"IT IS ALMOST LIKE A DREAM. THE NEW REICH HAS BEEN BORN. FOURTEEN YEARS OF WORK HAVE BEEN CROWNED WITH VICTORY. THE GERMAN REVOLUTION HAS BEGUN!"

– Joseph Goebbels, Chief Propogandist of the Nazi Party

Adolf Hitler next set his sights on becoming Chancellor; he turned his attention to gaining support from large industrialists, members of the armed forces, and bankers. These groups of people reasoned that if they supported the Nazi Party and helped it gain power, the Party would, in turn, look after them. A reasonable assumption, perhaps. But these people failed to realize that Adolf Hitler was not the average politician and that he was unlikely to play by traditional political rules.

In early February 1932, President von Hindenberg began to show his true colors. He was further right on the political spectrum than previously had been thought. He signed a decree giving police the power to break up political rallies. His decree also banned associations and shut down selected media outlets. In June 1932, he appointed

Franz von Papen (National People's Party) to the office of Chancellor, replacing Heinrich Brüning.

However, von Papen struggled to garner respect in the Reichstag. His far-right ideas did not resonate with many politicians, aside from those representing the Nazi Party. For example, one executive order von Papen issued opened the way for the creation of Special Courts to "obliterate elements hostile to the State."

Hitler was furious. He could not tolerate any competition to his ideas and ideals. He could not have someone else doing the things that he had long dreamed of. The Nazi Party urged a non-confidence motion in the Reichstag. By a narrow margin, von Papen survived the vote but only a few months later, he lost a second non-confidence motion. His political career was over. President von Hindenberg replaced him with General Kurt von Schleicher. Von Hindenberg and von Schleicher were cut from the same cloth in that they both envisioned an authoritarian regime to rule Germany.

Competition from von Papen was one matter. Now there was von Schleicher to deal with. Adolf Hitler would have none of it. He could not tolerate the notion of someone else embracing his ideas. In 1932, he ran for the office of President. He lost the election, but his meticulously organized campaign of speeches at rallies further strengthened his popularity. Six million Germans were still without work and many others were still struggling economically.

Aware of the growing appeal of the Nazi Party, in 1933, former Chancellor von Papen decided to support the Nazi Party and began to pressure President von Hindenburg to appoint Hitler as the Chancellor of Germany. Nineteen of the large industrialists who supported the Nazi Party signed a petition demanding that von Hindenberg make Adolf Hitler the Chancellor. President von Hindenberg might have taken stock of the instability in the Reichstag with its many small, minority Parties and reasoned that Hitler, as Chancellor, would see to it that the Nazi Party cooperated with these minority Parties to ensure political stability.

Behind the scenes, however, a different reason was unfolding. President von Hindenberg was 86 years old, fading into senility, and easily influenced. Nazi Party members had been quietly threatening Von Hindenberg with Article 59 of the Constitution which said that 100 Reichstag members could propose (and a 2/3 majority could affirm) a motion to prosecute the President for illegal actions undertaken while in Office. What evidence they had against him is not clear. Cornered and unable to push back against the aggressors, on January 30, 1933 President von Hindenberg asked Chancellor von Schleicher to resign. Adolf Hitler was then made the Chancellor of Germany.

The avowed hater of Jews who had at one time survived by doing menial labour while living in a men's shelter and eating at soup kitchens was now the Chancellor of Germany.

Chancellor Hitler made sure that his *Schutzstaffel* (SS) took every available opportunity to march through the streets of German towns and cities. Curious onlookers would crowd the sidewalks for a glimpse of the spectacle. In Berlin, Chancellor Hitler could often be seen looking out his window as SS troops marched by. His arm could be seen repeatedly saluting the SS troops with his characteristic open-handed salute. Hitler bragged to those around him that his political philosophy (now called the Third Reich) would endure for a thousand years. In hindsight, we know now that his estimation was stretched. But the people who aligned themselves with the Nazi Party were not bothering to question his future predictions. They were too busy blindly following Adolf Hitler's every move.

As the newly minted Chancellor, Hitler swiftly moved to widen the circle of ruthless and loyal men around him: Rudolf Hess, Julius Streicher, Gregor Strasser, Ernst Röhm, Hermann Göring, Wilhelm Frick, Heinrich Himmler, and Joseph Goebbels. Hess and Streicher were loyal disciples but lacked the talent to be of assistance to Hitler. Strasser and Röhm would go on to play key roles in managing the radical element of the Nazi Party. Röhm would also look after the SS troops. Strasser would head up the office of Political Organization. Göring (former SA head) would play a leadership role in the German Air Force. Göring was also tasked with creating a secret police service. Frick, a former policeman devoutly loyal to Hitler's cause, handled less-challenging tasks. Himmler, a former poultry farmer with a degree in agronomy, would become a mastermind behind racial policy and the running of concentration camps. Goebbels would become Chief Propogandist and would create the Ministry of Enlightenment and People's Propaganda. This Ministry brought the media to heel; all forms of media including radio, film, literature, music and art were ordered to support the Nazi Party philosophy and policies.

Chancellor Hitler even went so far as to ensure the Nazi Party had an official song. The song adopted had been created by Party supporter Horst Wessel - the son of a Protestant Minister. Wessel had forsaken his upbringing and spent his days attending Nazi Party gatherings and consorting with prostitutes in Berlin. Prior to being murdered by a gang of Communists, Wessel had penned a song which he called *Kampflied* (the fight song). Hitler was so moved by the song and by Wessel's dedication to the Party that he decided to adopt the song as the official song of the Nazi Party.

Chancellor Hitler turned his attention to the media and to the judiciary. Building on the efforts of Goebbels, he shut down all opposition newspapers and jailed journalists who had a left-leaning philosophy. His disdain for judges led to the creation of the People's

Supreme Court (*Volksgerichtshof*) which would focus on enemies of the State. Thousands of such enemies would be tried by this Court and many of them sentenced to death.

On the night of February 27, 1933, the Reichstag parliamentary building mysteriously caught fire and was destroyed. The Nazis argued the fire was evidence that Communist agitators were plotting against the German government. The Nazi Party then conveniently arrested a mentally-challenged Dutch Communist sympathizer, Marinus van der Lubbe, who was known to have a fascination with fire. After a speedy trial, he was declared guilty, and decapitated. Was Göring behind it? Was Goebbels behind it? The answer will never be known.

However, the fire did provide Chancellor Hitler a convenient opportunity to pressure President von Hindenburg into signing the *Reichstag Fire Decree* -- an order that suspended civil liberties across the country. Political opponents could now be arrested and jailed without specific charges.

But Hitler wanted more. On March 23, 1933, in a powerful speech to parliament (which was now meeting in the Berlin Opera House), Chancellor Hitler made his case for the passage of the *Enabling Act* which gave him, as Chancellor, the power to make and enforce laws without the involvement of the parliament or President von Hindenburg.

His powerful oratory was compelling and the Act was passed. Adolf Hitler now began to remake the German political system, doing away with freedom of speech, the press, and legal due process. The German Constitution was gutted.

ABSOLUTE POWER

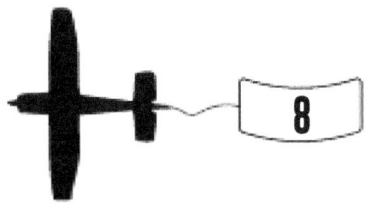

With the *Enabling Act* giving him unbridled power, Adolf Hitler wasted little time in remaking Germany in his autocratic vision of a nation cleansed of socially and racially tainted groups. Labour unions were dissolved. Opposition political Parties were ordered dissolved. Suspected Communists were arrested. Social Democrat rallies were forcibly halted by SS troops. He encouraged German citizens to boycott retail shops owned by Jews. SS troops burned books at Jewish-funded universities. Thousands of Jews were arrested. Tyranny ruled the streets. Police, local government authorities, and individual citizens all participated in discriminatory efforts to support the racial health of Germany and to support the views of Adolf Hitler and the Third Reich.

RÖHM MAKES A MOVE

SS boss Ernst Röhm decided to make a play for power. The remaining fragments of the SA combined with the now powerful SS comprised over two million men. Röhm boldly suggested that the SA and SS be combined and placed under command of a Ministry of Defence to be headed up by himself. The German military was alarmed at this idea; a development that placed Chancellor Hitler in a difficult position. He could not have the German military angry at him over Röhm's idea. Röhm encouraged SA leaders to start interfering with local government affairs. This threatened to make Hitler look weak to his inner circle of supporters. The industrialists who had been supporting the Nazi Party started calling for an end to the persecution of Jews and an end to the looting of churches. As tensions around him mounted, Hitler began fearing that some of his inner circle were poised to turn against him. The Nazi Party had come this far. As far as Adolf Hitler was concerned, there could be no turning back now. He had to control the narrative.

HITLER RESPONDS

Hitler plotted his next moves carefully. He first had to calm the fears of the military. He could not have the military brass think that he was a weak Chancellor. In early April 1934, he accompanied the Army and Navy on exercises in East Prussia. He used this opportunity to draw himself closer to the military commanders. He suggested to them that when von Hindenberg eventually passed away, the military brass should support a Hitler bid for the Presidency.

To demonstrate to the miliary commanders that he was a strong leader, Adolf Hitler concocted a story that the SA under direction from Ernst Röhm was planning a coup. He suggested to the miliary leaders that they watch how he dealt with this threat. During the first couple days of July 1934, the *Schutzstaffel* (SS) under the direction of

Heinrich Himmler received orders from Hitler to kill key members of the SA. In addition, he ordered the killing of any members of the Nazi Party whom he felt might one day pose a threat to his grip on power. These figures included Gregor Strasser, Erich Klausner (head of the Catholic Action group), Bavarian politician Gustav Ritter von Kahr, and of course Ernst Röhm. It is estimated that over 150 SA individuals were eliminated by Himmler's and Göring's firing squads in what the history books now call the "Night of the Long Knives".

Adolf Hitler's grip on power was now unchallenged. In late 1934, he declared himself Party leader for life. From then through 1938, he effectively took control of the Reichstag by ordering a reduction in the number of parliamentary sessions. In response to his bloody purge of the SA, the military commanders sat by in stunned silence as Hitler anointed himself the Supreme Commander of the armed forces. He seized the bank accounts of trade unions, threw union leaders in prison, seized control of churches, took over schools, and muzzled the press. The conversion of Germany to a dictatorship was complete. Adolf Hitler could now create a mighty military machine and focus on the conquest of other countries.

Through this final grab for complete power, he maintained a high degree of captivation over the German people by carefully curating a sense of power. He staged mass marches of SS and military troops through the streets of German cities. To embellish the atmosphere, he made use of marching bands dressed in uniforms. In reality, he had little to offer but the people continued to buy into his perceived aura of charismatic power.

Behind the scenes, Hitler began formulating plans to expand the use of concentration camps. He ordered Heinrich Himmler to proceed with the construction of new camps modeled on the one at Dachau.

He also began defining new reasons for arresting and detaining people who still might be opposed to him.

> "I NOTED HOW PEOPLE LOOKED. THEIR FACES FULL OF BIBLICAL DEVOTION, AS IF DELIRIOUS, THEY STRETCHED OUT THEIR ARMS AND GREETED HIM WITH SCREAMS AND SHOUTS OF 'HEIL HITLER'. "

– Karl Otto Schmidt, German psychologist and writer

By October 1934, Hitler had added 300,000 troops to the army's ranks. He ordered a start to the construction of submarines, a move which the *Treaty of Versailles* strictly forbade. He established the *League of Air Sports*, not for sporting, but for training military pilots.

He realized that Germany needed two critical raw materials if it was to one day wage war: gasoline and rubber. The Nazi Party gave orders to German manufacturing company I.G. Farben to ramp up the output of synthetic fuel made from lignite coal gasification using the "Fischer Tropsch" process. This mandate's target was for an output of 300,000 tons a year by 1937. Orders were also given to I.G. Farben to ramp up the output of synthetic rubber for eventual use in tires for military vehicles.

FRENCH AND BRITISH INACTION

In spite of Hitler's growing geopolitical threat, the political leaders of other countries did nothing to publicly criticize what was happening in Germany. In particular, France and Britain were focused on Abyssinia (present day Ethiopia) where Mussolini was making progress in taking over the area.

Hitler decided to make a gamble. He was convinced that Britain and France were so preoccupied with the Abyssinia situation that they would scarcely notice what was happening in Germany. On March 2, 1936, Hitler ordered General Blomberg to advance three battalions of German troops into the Rhineland area (present day areas of Bonn, Cologne, Dusseldorf, and Essen); a move which was expressly forbidden by the *Treaty of Versailles*.

On March 16, 1935, Hitler instituted a decree that made military service mandatory for 500,000 men. This was another blatant violation of the *Treaty of Versailles*. Britain protested this move, but did little else to stop it. French General Gamelin tepidly moved several of his troop divisions forward, but that was all.

Had the French troops taken more decisive action against the German battalions then and there, the arc of world history might have been favourably shifted. Instead, the failure of the French troops to engage elevated Hitler's ego. His Rhineland gamble had just paid off handsomely; France's reputation amongst other European nations had been dealt a mighty blow.

AUSTRIA AND CZECHOSLOVAKIA FALL

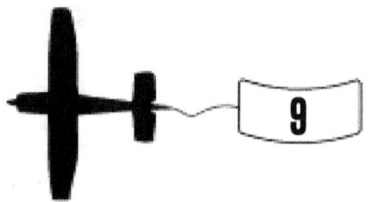

In October 1936, Hitler gave Hermann Göring, Commander-in-Chief of the Luftwaffe (air force), a mandate to prepare Germany for war. Göring was well suited for this assignment. He had been an ace fighter pilot in World War I, was devoted to the Nazi cause, and was the architect of the Gestapo Secret Police (*Geheime Staatspolizei*). The mandate of the Gestapo was to protect the Nazi movement from political enemies by using informants, interrogation, and even brutal torture. Göring further used the Gestapo to ban Jews from movie cinemas, museums, fairs, lecture halls, and swimming pools. Jews were even banned from driving. As Göring orchestrated actions of the Gestapo with the full knowledge and backing of Adolf Hitler, the rest of the world sat idly by.

Unchallenged by world leaders, Hitler devoted all of 1937 to training troops, amassing synthetic fuel, and stockpiling rubber; all while keeping a watchful eye on the politics in Britain and France.

MCKENZIE KING – BAMBOOZLED?

In June 1937, Canadian Prime Minister William Lyon McKenzie King attended the coronation of King George VI. Following the coronation festivities, McKenzie King decided to pay a visit to Adolf Hitler. King's diary suggests he was impressed with Hitler.

> "WHEN I WAS FORMALLY SHOWN INTO THE ROOM WHERE HERR HITLER RECEIVED ME, HE WAS WEARING EVENING DRESS. QUIETLY AND PLEASANTLY, HE SAID HE WAS PLEASED TO SEE ME IN GERMANY. HIS FACE IS MUCH MORE PREPOSSESSING THAN HIS PICTURES GIVE THE IMPRESSION OF. IT IS NOT THAT OF A FIREY, OVERSTRAINED NATURE, BUT OF A CALM, PASSIVE MAN DEEPLY AND THOUGHTFULLY EARNEST. HIS SKIN WAS SMOOTH. HIS FACE DID NOT PRESENT LINES OF WEARINESS. HIS EYES IMPRESSED ME MOST OF ALL. HIS EYES HAD A LIQUID QUALITY ABOUT THEM WHICH SUGGESTED A KEEN PERCEPTION AND A PROFOUND SYMPATHY."

– William Lyon McKenzie King
Prime Minister of Canada 1935-1944

Was he impressed? Or, had he been bamboozled? King explained to Hitler that in the event of war, Canada would voluntarily step in to assist Britain. Hitler assured King that there would be no war. After their conversation wrapped up, King left the meeting carrying a signed portrait of Hitler mounted in a silver frame. King believed the two were on track for a genuine friendship.

To further appreciate McKenzie King's position, one must consider that he had been Prime Minister of Canada from 1921 to 1930. The crash of Wall Street in 1929 set the global economy on a trajectory towards economic depression. King's Liberal government was slow to respond to the crisis, feeling that the economy would quickly bounce back. This laissez-faire attitude cost the Party its grip on power in the 1930 general election. However, Conservative Prime Minister R.B. Bennett could not manage to stem the economic bleeding either and in the 1935 election McKenzie King's Liberals were returned to power.

This taste of how the electorate could suddenly bounce a Party out of power no doubt unsettled McKenzie King. He was acutely aware that talk of war would raise the thorny issue of conscription. English-speaking Canadians were generally in favour of conscription; French-speaking Canadians, definitely not. Talk of war could divide the Liberal caucus and indeed the entire nation. King was determined to keep any talk of war to a minimum. If war was to occur, it should be fought in the air, not with boots on the ground, not with conscripted men.

THE BRITISH RAF - REBUFFED

In the British general election of June 1935, the Conservative Party under the leadership of Stanley Baldwin was returned to power. With Britain also feeling the effects of the global economic depression, Baldwin opted for a position of appeasement with Germany. He convinced the British people that there was no reason to be alarmed over the rantings and ravings of Adolf Hitler.

What was not apparent to the British people is that in late in 1935, the British government had approached the McKenzie King government to discuss the potential for training Royal Air Force (RAF) pilots in Canada. This overture was soundly rebuffed. Although McKenzie King was reluctant to say it out loud, he was not going to risk his political hide on talk of training pilots because of the actions of one man in Germany; a man whom he felt would one day be his friend.

AN IDEA TAKES ROOT

In July 1936, the British RAF created its "Volunteer Reserve Program" to train pilots on weekends at civilian airfields. However, this training effort proved largely ineffective; the weather was often foul which curtailed flight training hours and the runways at the civilian airfields were nothing more than grass landing strips that quickly turned to mud when it rained.

As the shortcomings of this training program became evident, Robert Leckie, a staff member to RAF Air Commodore Arthur Tedder, proposed the idea that flight training efforts be moved to Canada. After all, Canada was a colony and would not push back against such a scheme. Or would it?

When Prime Minister McKenzie King was apprised of Leckie's training scheme, he once more bristled with concern. English-speaking Canadians would no doubt be in favour of the RAF training their pilots in Canada. French-speaking Canadians would most certainly be opposed to the idea. King reasoned that the political fallout from such a training plan could cost him the next election. Leckie's idea was rejected.

By mid-1937, the RAF Volunteer Reserve Program had only managed to create nine flight training schools and train 247 pilots. While these tepid numbers were influenced by weather and infrastructure, it also seems there was a lack of urgency to the effort which was likely aided by British politicians still fixated on appeasing Adolf Hitler.

However, as Hitler became more belligerent, a sense of urgency finally materialized among King's inner circle. They quietly agreed that Canada would send 15 officer cadets and 25 seasoned officers to

Britain in each of the coming years to serve in the RAF. Each would be given elementary flight training before departing for Britain. In addition, Australia, New Zealand, southern Rhodesia, and Kenya also agreed to participate in the program. This was the genesis of what would eventually become the British Commonwealth Air Training Plan (BCATP).

AUSTRIA FALLS

World leaders were unaware that Hitler had concocted plans to conquer Austria. On February 16, 1938, Adolf Hitler summoned Austrian Chancellor Kurt von Schuschnigg to a meeting in Berlin. For hours, Hitler condescendingly lectured von Schuschnigg. Hitler then presented him with a document calling for the Austrian parliament to turn the reins of government over to the German Nazi Party within one week. The agreement also called for Austria to afford a complete amnesty for any crimes that would be committed by the Nazis. Chancellor von Schuschnigg was told that if he did not sign the document, German troops would advance into Austria. Seeing no way out of the predicament, Chancellor von Schuschnigg signed the paper. Adolf Hitler had taken control of Austria without so much as a gunshot being fired. In a subsequent speech to the Reichstag, Hitler cynically spoke of Schuschnigg's warm understanding and willingness to bring Germany and Austria closer together.

With assistance from the SS and Gestapo, tens of thousands of Jewish men and women in Austria were jailed after being robbed of their properties, paintings, tapestries, and other valuables. Baron Louis de Rothschild was allowed to flee Vienna, but only after turning over his steel mills to German control. At the helm of this overall program of theft was Nazi Party supporter Karl Adolf Eichmann who invited German businessmen and bankers to buy up the properties taken from Austrian Jews who had been sent to a concentration camp.

Military assistance from Britain, France, Canada, or Russia could have easily thwarted Hitler's advance on Austria. But, these countries sat by and watched instead, silently hoping that Austria would be an isolated event.

SUDETENLAND GOES NEXT

Since the 9th century, the German-speaking regions of Bohemia, Moravia, and Silesia had been part of the Austro-Hungarian (Habsburg) empire. World War I spelled the end of the Austro-Hungarian empire and on October 18, 1918, the provisional nation of Czechoslovakia proclaimed its independence. The *Treaty of St. Germain* signed in September 1919 officially recognized the Republic of Czechoslovakia.

Hitler regarded the country as nothing more than an artificial construct that had been created by peace treaties. At issue was the estimated 3.25 million German speaking people who mostly resided in the vicinity of the Sudeten Mountains (an area referred to as *Sudetenland*). The dominant political Party in the Sudetenland was the Sudeten German Party, which was closely aligned with the German Nazi Party. Hitler decided he was going to offer freedom to the people of Sudetenland.

BRITISH AND FRANCE – INDECISION

In March 1938, French Foreign Minister Joseph Paul-Boncour asked Britain for a commitment that should Germany invade Czechoslovakia and should France step in to help Czechoslovakia, that Britain would support France. Britain bureaucrats bluntly rejected this overture. Prime Minister Chamberlain and Viscount Halifax then suggested to France that the Sudetenland perhaps should be separated off from the rest of Czechoslovakia. French bureaucrats for a brief moment floated the idea of organizing a plebiscite so that the residents of the

Sudetenland could express their desire for separation. But they quickly capitulated on the idea.

GENERAL BECK BEGINS TO WORRY

With Britain and France tangled up in indecision, German Army Chief of Staff General Ludwig Beck started worrying about how Hitler was ignoring the concerns of his military leaders. Beck worried that Hitler's desire to take overt action against neighboring countries would eventually draw fire from Britain and France. He worried that a full-on European war might even come to involve the United States. Beck's concerns would eventually prove to be deadly accurate.

In discussing his worries with his fellow Generals, Beck realized that they too were frightened of Adolf Hitler. On August 19, 1938, Beck submitted his resignation, disgusted by the attitude of Adolf Hitler. Hitler accepted the resignation, but then demanded that Beck not speak a word of his resignation to the media. Out of fear for his life, Beck kept his mouth shut. Britain and France would not learn of his resignation for several more months.

THE SITUATION INTENSIFIES

In May 1938, the Czechoslovakian military began to mobilize troops and equipment to stave off what they felt was an imminent invasion by Germany. Diplomats from Britain, France, and Russia issued tersely-worded communiques to Hitler. The communiques inflamed him, but they also scared him enough that he momentarily backed down from his plan to invade Czechoslovakia.

After several days of deep thought, Hitler's rage re-surfaced and in an about-face he announced to his military commanders, "Czechoslovakia will be wiped off the map." The date he laid down for the invasion was October 1, 1938.

On September 12, 1938 Adolf Hitler delivered a blistering radio address from a rally in Nuremberg. He demanded an end to the oppression of Sudeten Germans. This speech stirred up a riot in Sudetenland, which the Czech army promptly put down by declaring martial law. The Cabinet of French Prime Minister Daladier met at length to decide if France would support Czechoslovakia in the event of a German invasion. No decision was made and the Cabinet remained divided. The British ambassador to France was summoned by the Cabinet and asked to contact Prime Minister Chamberlain. After an exchange of phone calls, Chamberlain announced that he would come to Germany the very next day to meet with Adolf Hitler.

THE MUNICH AGREEMENT

During his meeting with Chamberlain, Hitler focused on the plight of the three million German-speaking residents of the Sudetenland. Hitler demanded bluntly of Chamberlain that Britain throw its support behind carving out the Sudetenland from Czechoslovakia. Chamberlain advised Hitler that he essentially agreed to the idea in principle, but needed to consult with the British Cabinet first. In effect, the leader of Britain had just signaled to the leader of the Nazi Party that Britain was a weak nation that could not stand up against the Nazi Party.

On September 14, 1938, Chamberlain sent a cable to Hitler advising that a British delegation would be arriving in Germany the next day for discussions. The Czechs were incensed that they had not been invited. A portion of their country was at stake.

Hitler was now more than certain that Chamberlain was operating from a position of weakness. When Hitler met with the British delegation on September 15th, he pledged that he would not march on Czechoslovakia unless some outrageous incident forced his hand.

Prime Minister Chamberlain's comments in his diary from these days confirm his weakness. Chamberlain actually thought Hitler could be trusted.

"IN SPITE OF THE HARSHNESS AND RUTHLESSNESS IN HIS FACE, I THOUGH HERE WAS A MAN WHO COULD BE RELIED UPON WHEN HE HAD GIVEN HIS WORD".

– Neville Chamberlain, *Diary*

What Chamberlain did not quite grasp was that members of his own Party were turning against him because of his weak leadership abilities. On September 26, 1938, Conservative MP Leo Amery wrote an op-ed piece for *The Times* newspaper. His op-ed stated: *the issue has become very simple. Are we to surrender to ruthless brutality a free people whose cause we have espoused but are now to throw to the wolves to save our own skin, or are we still able to stand up to a bully? It is not Czechoslovakia but our own soul that is at stake.*

Despite Amery's criticism, Chamberlain still could not take a hard stance. He cabled Hitler to feebly say, "I feel certain that you can get all essentials without war, and without delay." Adolf Hitler then advised his military commanders to be ready for invasion. But two last-minute developments caused him to pause. Both the Kingdom of Yugoslavia and Rumania advised the Hungarian government they would attack Hungary if Germany attached Czechoslovakia. In an unusual moment of French decisiveness, a cable from Paris threatened to mobilize French troops if Germany made a move against Czechoslovakia.

This developments prompted Hitler to send hastily written cables to France, Britain, and Italy demanding that their delegates attend a meeting in Munich the next day (September 29, 1938) to settle the Sudetenland issue. At this meeting, Hitler sensed that France and Britain wanted to avoid war. He decided to manipulate them. He bluntly informed the delegates in attendance that the Czechoslovakian occupation would commence October 1 and would be complete by October 10.

On September 30, 1938, the leaders of France, Britain, and Italy overwhelmed by a desire to appease Hitler, buckled at the knees and affixed their signatures to the *Munich Agreement* which gave Hitler the green light to march troops into the Sudetenland.

Chamberlain then asked Hitler to sign a joint declaration stating that the *Munich Agreement* represented the symbolic desire of the Britain and Germany would never to go to war again. The French were deeply embarrassed at Chamberlain's request. Czechoslovakia was being forced to give up 11,000 square miles of its land, most of its coal mining, most of its chemical manufacturing, most of its steel mills, and a big portion of its power generation. And in response, Britain wanted a document signed attesting to never going to war with Germany. Chamberlain was a pathetic leader and so too was French Prime Minister Daladier; Hitler knew it.

Hitler had outplayed France and Britain and had embarrassed them both on the world stage. Later the next day, abandoned by Britain and France, Czechoslovakia surrendered. Hitler advanced troops into the country.

CHURCHILL TAKES A STAND

Upon returning to London, Chamberlain said "the settlement of the Czech problem... is in my view only the prelude to a larger settlement in which all Europe may find peace." As he walked into 10 Downing Street, he popped his head out of a first floor window and said to the crowd gathered outside, "My good friends, this is the second time in our history that there has come back from Germany to Downing Street peace with honour. I believe it is peace for our time." The British people were elated. Gifts and letters of praise poured into 10 Downing Street and Chamberlain's popularity soared.

Winston Churchill, former First Lord of the Admiralty, and now a backbench MP for the constituency of Epping, could not take it much longer. He lashed out against Chamberlain saying, "All that the *Munich Agreement* has changed is the German dictator. Instead of snatching his victuals from the table, he now has them served to him course by course. We have sustained a total, unmitigated defeat."

As the Sudetenland events played out, the British RAF had only two Spitfires and a handful of Hawker Hurricanes that were airworthy. Only 29 of 52 fighter squadrons were remotely ready for action. Scores of Gladiators, Furies, Gauntlets, and Demons sat in disrepair. In France, only 700 of 1,126 planes were operational. Of the ones operational, only 50 were modern.

These numbers were a drop in the bucket compared to the air power of the German Luftwaffe under the command of Hermann Göring: 2,760 planes, including 1,368 bombers. The invasion of Czechoslovakia had garnered a booty of 1.5 million rifles, 750 planes, 600 tanks, and 2,000 artillery guns. Germany was well on its way to having 4,000 aircraft and several hundred thousand support personnel at the ready.

KRISTALLNACHT

On November 7, 1938, a German employee at the German embassy in Paris was shot and killed by Herschel Grynszpan, a 17-year-old Polish Jew. In response, Adolf Hitler decided to unleash the power of the SS. Over a two-night span, 267 synagogues were torched, 7,500 Jewish-owned shops were smashed into and looted, Jewish homes were robbed and their occupants beaten. Some 30,000 Jewish men were rounded up and herded off to concentration camps at Dachau, Buchenwald, and Sachsenhausen.

CHAMBERLAIN'S AWAKENING

On March 17, 1939, British Prime Minister Chamberlan suddenly awoke from his blind stupor of appeasement to the grim reality of what was happening in Europe. Germany was creating a serious problem. He went on the political offensive to save his political hide.

On March 31, 1939, Chamberlain again addressed the German aggression issue. He promised that if Germany invaded Poland, Britain would step in to help Poland.

"IN THE EVENT OF ANY ACTION WHICH CLEARLY THREATENED POLISH INDEPENDENCE AND WHICH THE POLISH GOVERNMENT CONSIDERED IT VITAL TO RESIST WITH THEIR NATIONAL FORCES, HIS MAJESTY'S GOVERNMENT WOULD FEEL THEMSELVES BOUND TO LEND THE POLISH GOVERNMENT ALL SUPPORT IN THEIR POWER. I MAY ADD THAT THE FRENCH GOVERNMENT HAS AUTHORIZED ME TO MAKE IT PLAIN THAT THEY TAKE THE SAME POSITION."

– Neville Chamberlain, British Prime Minister

CANADA DITHERS WHILE HITLER ADVANCES

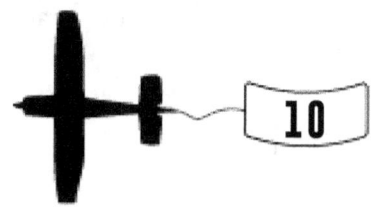

Prime Minister McKenzie King was acutely aware of the dangers posed by shifting political winds. His political future demanded that he avoid any reference to war and to the divisive issue of conscription. Following his June 1937 meeting with Adolf Hitler, McKenzie King openly expressed sentiment that Hitler was generally a good person and that there would be no war.

The Liberal MPs dutifully supported their leader. On February 16, 1937, Liberal MP Joseph Alphida-Crete (St. Maurice-Lafleche - Quebec) stood in the House of Commons and expressed the view that Canada was safe from conquest.

Social Credit MP Mr. Percy Rowe (Athabaska - Alberta) held a different opinion. He felt the world was on the verge of bloodshed because of the failure to form a *League of Nations*. He very eloquently stated, "The fear of war again burdens the world. Economic conflicts have multiplied. Hostile tariffs fetter world trade. Currencies are unstable. Nations are unable to buy goods which they need. Economic nationalism is rampant." He went on to explain that the economic weakness was due to the self-contradictory foundation of the League of Nations. It rested partly on fear, partly on fellowship, partly on a belief in armed force, and partly on hope for future tranquility. In a pointed jab at Woodrow Wilson, Lloyd George, and Georges Clemenceau, he stated, "because these men either would not or could not face cold realities and speak the plain truth, we have before us the old, old story, repeated so many times in the last ten thousand years of mankind's tribal warfare, of the victors, aided by their tribal deities, who are usually on the side of the heaviest artillery, standing over the body of a prostrate foe, dictating under duress and force, at the point of a sword held at the throat of the vanquished, a Treaty so full of injustices and economic contradictions that not only could it not live out a full year, it literally sowed the dragon's teeth which have sprung up in nazi-ism, fascism and war, finally bringing the world again to the brink of another deluge of blood."

As eloquent as Rowe's words were, Prime Minister McKenzie King could safely ignore him because the Social Credit Party held only 16 seats in the House of Commons. However, by the Spring of 1938, McKenzie King could no longer deny that the European situation was quickly deteriorating. Despite the positive sentiment radiating from British Prime Minister Neville Chamberlain, sideline discussions had begun between Britain and Canada over the subject of building more aircraft in Canada to support the British RAF. Although Chamberlain was denying it, Britain was growing painfully aware that war was in the offing.

The Opposition Conservatives had become aware of these discussions between Britain and Canada. On May 16, 1938, in the House of

Commons, they grilled Liberal Minister of Defence Ian Mackenzie on the subject of airplanes. He revealed that the Department of Defence had in fact contacted manufacturing firms in Canada to assess their ability to both manufacture parts for aircraft and to assemble aircraft. He further revealed that Canada was taking steps to acquire 203 aircraft for its own inventory. He conceded that with delivery dates for these aircraft spread out over the coming twelve months, Canada was in no way prepared to come to the aid of Britain if a war were to break out suddenly. Moreover, he noted that Canada only had 247 officers and 1,823 airmen at the ready. In other words, Canada was ill equipped to assist Britain in the event that war against Germany was declared.

By early 1939, Prime Minister McKenzie King was still hesitant to take a firm stance on helping Britain in the event of war. At the March 30, 1939 sitting of the House of Commons, the best the Prime Minister could offer was to say that he supported the efforts of British Prime Minister Chamberlain in his efforts to avert a war over the Czechoslovakia situation. He made it further clear that any decision on Canada engaging in war would be the decision of the entire Canadian parliament, not just his Liberal Cabinet.

The Opposition were also sitting on their hands. Instead of taking a firm position on the subject of war, the Conservative Party Leader, the Hon. R. J. Manion, deflected the issue onto the governing Liberals. He stated, "I have thus far refused to make any statement, not only because of the huge Liberal majority, but because the Prime Minister of Canada alone can speak with authority for this country. Certainly, no word of mine could be helpful, either to him or to the empire." He went on to say, " I can assure Mr. King that whatever steps he and the government take in support of Mr. Chamberlain and the empire will have the full cooperation of the Conservative party and its leader." In other words, the Conservatives were content to do nothing.

As Canadian politicians bounced the war issue around in the House of Commons, Germany continued to wreak havoc. The inaction by Canada and Britain played right into Adolf Hitler's hands. The Nazi Party took further steps to repress Catholic, Protestant, and Jewish liberties. Germany factories producing armaments were operating in high gear. Germany was fast approaching the point where it could adequately defend itself against attack by an aggressor nation.

The Sudetenland area recently taken from Czechoslovakia was now a German satellite state. Its foreign policies, political decisions, economic actions, railways, and roads were being controlled by Berlin. To gain more control, Hitler and his operatives in Czechoslovakia worked to foment local grievances. To quell the upset, more German troops were sent in and more control was exerted.

Adolf Hitler next had his eye on the geographic area between the Baltic Sea and the Mediterranean; an area comprising 100 million people all divided by race, creed, old feuds, and new ambitions. This geographic swath was undeveloped industrially, but had the agricultural, timber, and mineral resources that Germany needed to further extend its power. Beyond these states lay an even bigger prize, the rich agricultural fields of the Ukraine.

But first, he made an all-too-familiar move on Rumania (present day Romania). He presented the Rumanian government with an ultimatum: allow Germany to advantage itself of Rumania's agricultural output – or else! The Rumanian parliament caved and allowed Germany to gain monopoly control over large quantities of agricultural produce. In addition, permission was granted for Germany to develop oilfields, build roads, and construct power plants.

Hitler next rolled out this same strategy in Lithuania. In short order, the Lithuanian parliament agreed to cede the Memel region of the country back to Germany. This region had been part of Germany prior to the *Treaty of Versailles*.

It seemed there was no stopping Adolf Hitler.

WAR !

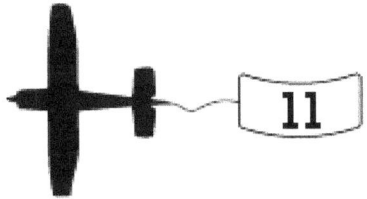

11

After hearing Chamberlain's position on Poland, Hitler flew into a rage. On April 3, 1939 he issued a directive to his military commanders regarding an invasion of Poland: "Preparations must be made so that the operation can be carried out any time from September 1, 1939."

Days after this April 3rd directive, Italy's Mussolini invaded Albania. France and Britain responded with a guarantee of help for neighboring Greece and Rumania. One month later, Mussolini and Hitler entered into a pact. Article III of the pact stated: *If one of the High Contracting Parties should become involved in warlike complications with another High Power, the other High Contracting Party would immediately come to its assistance with all its military forces.*

POLAND FALLS

On May 23, 1939, Hitler summoned his military commanders to a meeting. Hitler's adjutant (military assistant) was present and his hand-written notes that survived reveal that Hitler spoke about how it was now impossible to acquire more territory without the shedding of blood. He made it clear that his strategy would be to deal a crushing blow to Poland and then go on to take Belgium, France, and Holland. This would then lead to a successful war against Britain. Hitler's only fear was that Russia might form a military alliance with Britain and France.

However, this fear would soon prove unfounded. Seeking to protect himself from any German aggression, Russian leader Josef Stalin entered into a non-aggression pact with Germany. Terms of the pact called for neither side to attack the other. They agreed to partition Poland and to jointly influence the Baltic states.

By late July, Russia had started to fear that Germany would not adhere to the terms of the non-aggression pact. Russia reached out to Britain and France to engage in strategic discussions about how to manage an aggressive move by German forces. A group of bureaucrats was assembled and sent to Russia to begin talks. In a display of complete inefficiency, the group was sent via a passenger-cargo ship which made several port stops along the way. By the time the delegation arrived in Moscow on August 11, it was too little, too late. While the bureaucrats dithered on the slow-moving cargo ship, Hitler had ordered *Operation Himmler* to commence.

Under this operation, the German Gestapo obtained 150 Polish military uniforms, rounded up 150 condemned men from a concentration camp and outfitted them in the uniforms. These men were then ordered to attack a German radio station broadcast facility near the Polish border. Hitler would then argue that the Polish military had been responsible for the attack and that Germany had reason to invade Poland.

On August 25, 1939, the German cruiser Schleswig-Holstein arrived in the port of Danzig (today, Gdansk, Poland). The official story was that it was there to mark the anniversary of the German victory in the *Battle of Tannenberg* in World War I. As flags flew on deck and sailors stood at attention, over 200 marines hidden below deck were preparing for an unprovoked attack against Poland.

That same day, the British ambassador to Germany unexpectedly called on Adolf Hitler. In a further show of British weakness, the ambassador said that Britain was committed to the continued existence of the Nazi Party. He suggested that Britain and Germany sign a non-aggression pact. Hitler suggested he was interested, but only after he had dealt with the German-Polish problem.

If the weak-kneed British ambassador had instead forcefully pressed the issue then and there and persuaded Hitler to sign a non-aggression pact could the arc of world history have taken a different twist?

At 4:45 a.m. on the morning of September 1, 1939, Schleswig-Holstein's guns opened fire on the Port of Danzig, Poland. German troops flooded across the border and headed towards Warsaw. The British and French governments sent tersely worded ultimatums to Germany. Hitler ignored them. Later that night, German submarine U-30 torpedoed and sank the British liner *Athenia* as it sailed west of the Scottish Hebrides Isles.

This was a tipping point. Two days later, on September 3, the United Kingdom declared war on Germany. With news that the Polish air force had been destroyed and the Polish army was crumbling, France also declared war on Germany. The seeds planted by the *Treaty of Versailles* were beginning to bloom; World War II was underway.

CANADA STEPS UP

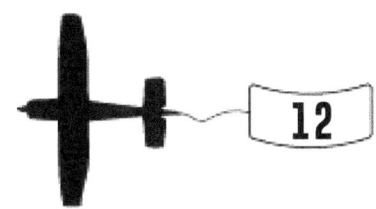

In early September 1939, as Poland crumbled, the Canadian parliament was still prorogued. It was not due to sit until October 2. However, the situation in Europe, now grave, demanded an early return to the House of Commons. On September 1, McKenzie King issued the following statement to the press: *It is now apparent that the efforts which have been made to preserve the peace of Europe are likely to prove of no avail. In spite of these efforts, hostilities have begun between Germany and Poland which threaten the peace of the world. The cabinet met at nine o'clock this morning and in accordance with the intimation given some days ago, decided to have parliament summoned forthwith. A proclamation has been issued summoning parliament to meet on Thursday, September 7.*

Support soon arrived from the provinces. The Premier of Saskatchewan sent the following telegram to the Prime Minister:

BOMBS AWAY!

REGINA, SASKATCHEWAN. SEPT. 2, 1939: MAY I ASSURE YOU OF THE SINCERE AND WHOLEHEARTED COOPERATION OF THE GOVERNMENT OF THIS PROVINCE IN ANY PLAN THE FEDERAL GOVERNMENT MAY EVOLVE TO GIVE EFFECTIVE COOPERATION TO GREAT BRITAIN IN THE PRESENT CRISIS. I CAN ASSURE YOU OF THE UNDIVIDED SUPPORT OF THE PEOPLE OF THE PROVINCE OF SASKATCHEWAN IN ANY ACTION THAT MAY BE AUTHORIZED BY THE PARLIAMENT OF CANADA.

– W. J. Patterson, Premier of Saskatchewan

The House of Commons convened on September 7 with the sitting lasting until September 13. Ever the careful politician concerned about re-election, McKenzie King made it clear that Canada was its own country. It would make decisions in its own good time, not when Mother Britain said so. He stated, "The action being taken by this country is voluntarily, not because of any colonial or inferior status vis-à-vis Great Britain, but because of an equality of status. We are a nation in the fullest sense, a member of the British Commonwealth of nations, sharing like freedom with Britain herself, a freedom which we believe we must all combine to save."

He concluded by saying, "What this world is facing today is deception, terror, violence and force, by a ruthless and tyrannical power which seeks world domination. I say there has not been a time, the period of the last war not excepted, when the countries of the world have faced such a crisis as they face today. I want to ask Honourable members and the people of Canada: In what spirit are you going to face this crisis? Are you going to face it believing in the rights of individuals, believing in the sacredness of human personality, believing in the freedom of nations, believing in all the sanctities of human life? I believe you are. I believe that through their representatives in this parliament, the Canadian people will so indicate in no uncertain way."

As per parliamentary protocol, MPs then walked to the Senate chamber to listen to the remarks of the Governor General (John Buchan, 1st Baron, Lord Tweedsmuir of Elsfield). The Governor General revealed that there was a statute on the books in Canada that allowed the government to take action outside of parliament – the *War Measures Act*. The *Act* had first been passed by the Parliament of Canada on August 22, 1914 and was contained in the *Statutes of Canada* as Chapter 206.

He said, "Honourable Members of the Senate and Members of the House of Commons: As you are only too well aware, all efforts to maintain the peace of Europe have failed. The United Kingdom, in honouring pledges given as a means of avoiding hostilities, has become engaged in war with Germany. You have been summoned at the earliest moment in order that the government may seek authority for the measures necessary for the defence of Canada, and for co-operation in the determined effort which is being made to resist further aggression, and to prevent the appeal to force instead of to pacifist means in the settlement of international disputes. Already the militia, the naval service and the air force have been placed on active service, and certain other provisions have been made for the defence of our coasts and our internal security under the *War Measures Act* and other existing authority. Proposals for further effective action by Canada will be laid before you without delay."

The following day, September 8, 1939, the House of Commons met to vote on a motion to accept the remarks of the Governor General. Parliamentary procedure called for a member of the governing Party to make a motion to accept the remarks of the Governor General. This task fell to H.S. Hamilton (Liberal MP for Algoma West).

In his speech supporting the motion, Hamilton provided emotional support for Canada's participation in the war when he said, "Mr.

Speaker, to me this war is Canada's war. To me the defeat of Britain is the defeat of Canada; the defeat of France is the defeat of Canada. In recent days, I have asked myself many times who lives, if England dies? Who dies, if England lives? Yes, and who lives if France dies; who dies if France lives?

The motion was seconded by J.A. Blanchette (Liberal MP for the Quebec riding of Compton). To ensure that the various Quebec Members of Parliament would be in favor of Canada going to war, Blanchette placed the topic of conscription front and center. He said, "I wish to state, without the slightest hesitation and without any mental reservation, that I am fully opposed to conscription. I am completely against a system so inconsistent with our Canadian turn of mind. Experience has shown, moreover, that it is not effective, for, without having given the desired results, it has, in the past, fostered trouble and unsettled our national life."

Opposition Leader Robert Manion threw his Party's support behind the Governor General's remarks saying: "…the Prime Minister has the assent and support of the party which I have the honour to lead. It is our duty to let the world, friends and foes alike, know that we are to-day unitedly behind the mother country in this war for human liberty."

Manion added "… we are fighting today for our conception of civilization and have no quarrel with the German people as a people. But Germany is controlled at the present time by an unscrupulous egoist. If Hitler and his philosophy conquer the world, civilization itself is likely to disappear, and the liberties for which our ancestors fought for a thousand years will go with it. Let us remember that if the democracies fall, Canada is the richest prize among the nations of the world. We should remember as well that this Canada of ours is very vulnerable to attack in these ultra-scientific days. If some nation should defeat England and France, the battle ground might well be at our own gates instead of being three thousand miles away across the Atlantic, as it is today. I submit that our best defence is an offensive in those far-off lands."

To set the stage for what was to come, the Prime Minister then quoted a couple key lines from a speech that Adolf Hitler had given in the Reichstag in 1935. He stressed that Hitler was erratic, — having once purported to be on the side of peace and now behaving as an aggressor.

"The German Reich—and in particular the present German government— have no other wish than to live on friendly and peaceful terms with all neighbouring states. We entertain these feelings not only towards the larger states, but also towards the neighbouring smaller states."

"Germany has nothing to gain by a European war of any kind. What we want is freedom and independence. For this reason, we were ready to conclude pacts of non-aggression with all our neighbours."

McKenzie King apprised the House of Commons that he had sent a telegram to Adolf Hitler on August 25, 1939. The telegram read: *The people of Canada are of one mind in believing that there is no international problem which cannot be settled by conference and negotiation. They equally believe that force is not a substitute for reason, and that the appeal to force as a means of adjusting international differences defeats rather than furthers the ends of justice. They are prepared to join what authority and power they may possess to that of the other nations of the British commonwealth in seeking a just and equitable settlement of the great problems with which nations are faced. On behalf of the Canadian people, but equally in the interests of humanity itself, I join with those of other countries and powers who have appealed to you, in the firm hope that your great power and authority will be used to prevent impending catastrophe by having recourse to every possible peaceful means to effect a solution of the momentous issues of this period of transition and change in world affairs.*

On Saturday, September 9, 1939, in the House of Commons, the Prime Minister made clear the next steps, "I should like to make clear to the House the procedure which the government has in mind as to giving effect to the decision of parliament regarding Canadian participation in the war. The adoption of the motion to accept the *Speech from the Throne* will be considered as approving the government's policy of immediate participation in the war. If the *Address in Reply to the Speech from the Throne* is approved, the government will immediately take steps for the issue of a formal proclamation of the existence of a state of war between Canada and the German Reich."

On September 9, 1939, the Senate passed an *Address in Reply to the Speech from the Throne.* The next day, Sunday, September 10, 1939, the House of Commons passed an *Address in Reply to the Speech from the Throne.*

The government of William Lyon McKenzie King now had the authority to declare war against Germany.

Following this session, the Cabinet recommended that a petition be submitted to His Majesty the King seeking authorization by him to issue a proclamation in the *Canada Gazette* declaring that a state of war with the German Reich exists and has existed in Canada from September 10, 1939.

The petition quickly received approval from the Governor General. The Canadian High Commissioner in London was instructed by telegram to submit to His Majesty a petition approving a war proclamation. A short while later, the Secretary of State for External

Affairs was informed by the Canadian High Commissioner that His Majesty had given his approval to the war proclamation.

As of September 13, 1939, the *War Measures Act* was in effect. Under the *War Measures Act*, the powers of the McKenzie King government extended to:

(a) Censorship and the control and suppression of publications, writings, maps, plans, photographs, communications and means of communication;

(b) Arrest, detention, exclusion and deportation;

(c) Control of the harbours, ports and territorial waters of Canada and the movements of vessels;

(d) Control of transportation by land, air, or water and the control of the transport of persons and things;

(e) Control over trading, exportation, importation, production and manufacture;

(f) Appropriation, control, forfeiture and disposition of property and of the use thereof.

The Governor General then concluded this sitting of parliament by saying, "I thank you in the name of His Majesty the King for the manner in which you have responded to the demands of this critical time. In enacting measures necessary for the defence of Canada you have performed a primary national obligation. In providing voluntarily for effective co-operation by Canada at the side of Britain and France in a war to resist aggression, you have made a momentous decision. The promptness with which you have acted affords unmistakable evidence of the ability of a free people, through its representatives in a free Parliament, to meet the grave emergencies of war."

Prime Minister McKenzie King had kept his promise that a war decision would be made by the entire House of Commons and not just his Liberal Party. However, after securing a war declaration, the House of Commons was prorogued. McKenzie King was reticent to risk his political survival by taking more overt steps.

THE BCATP

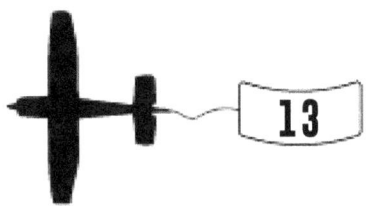

As Hitler's troops continued to create mayhem and destruction, the Canadian parliament remained prorogued. It was not until January 25, 1940 that MPs returned to the House of Commons where they were apprised of the developments over the past several months.

The Prime Minister revealed to the Commons that back on September 26, 1939, the British government had tabled a project plan involving the governments of Canada, Australia, and New Zealand to provide an ever-increasing flow of trained pilots, air observers, and air gunners to supplement the British RAF. Under the plan, airmen would be recruited and given elementary flight training in their respective countries. They would be given advanced training in Canada and then dispatched to Britain to assist the RAF. McKenzie King explained that he had presented the plan to his Cabinet who had accepted it in principle only.

He further revealed that on October 14, 1939, Lord Riverdale, a British aristocrat, had arrived in Ottawa to finalize the details of the plan. Lord Riverdale had shocked the Canadian bureaucrats with a grandiose set of plan details. He envisioned training 29,000 pilots/air observers/wireless air gunners a year and establishing seventy training schools across Canada. Three of these would be Bombing and Gunnery Schools. Canada's Air Commodore E.W. Stedman had put a price tag on Riverdale's plan of $888,500,000. Hearing this figure, Riverdale suggested Britain would pay $140,000,000 in-kind through contributions of planes and spare parts; the balance of $748,500,000 would be divided between Canada, Australia, and New Zealand with Canada's portion being $374,250,000.

McKenzie King explained that he and his Finance Minister had pushed back against this allocation arguing that such figures would bleed Canada to death economically. He explained that the only way these figures would work was if Britain agreed to substantially increase the amount of wheat it bought from Canada and if Canada reduced the amount of financial credit it extended to Britain. Lord Riverdale had reluctantly agreed to these terms. When Australia and New Zealand weighed in with cost concerns of their own, Riverdale reduced the scope of the plan to satisfy their delegates.

King detailed that under Riverdale's revised plan (which would be in effect through to March 31, 1943), Britain would supply over 1,300 twin-engine Avro Ansons, 750 Fairey Battles, 533 Harvards, plus half of the engines for the Tiger Moths. Canada would supply 187 Harvards, Tiger Moth airframes, and various other parts. The final bottom line figure of the aircraft portion of the plan was calculated at $607,271,210. Britain would make in-kind payments of $185,000,000 and Canada would provide $287,179,331. Adding in the training costs of $374,250,000 meant Canada's total contribution would be $661,429,331. By late November 1939, some effort had been applied to identifying locations for the various training facilities even though the actual plan still had not been signed and sealed.

McKenzie King then explained that he next demanded that all Canadian personnel trained as part of the air plan and dispatched overseas would be identified as being part of the RCAF and not the British RAF. Lord Riverdale and the British delegates expressed displeasure at this notion and the entire plan nearly fell apart. After a flurry of back and forth discussions between Ottawa and London, the British conceded on the issue of RCAF identity. He concluded his update to the House of Commons by noting that the air training plan had been signed on December 17, 1939. It would be called the British Commonwealth Air Training Plan (BCATP).

A FRESH MANDATE

Since the last sitting in September 1939, McKenzie King had done some soul searching. His political instincts were on high alert. On one hand, he realized that the Quebec section of his Liberal caucus would be in favor of the BCATP because it did not involve conscription – an issue the Province of Quebec was dead set against. On the other hand, he feared that the rest of his caucus might be uneasy about the BCATP because it did not involve large battalions of men. It would be a new way of participating in war; one that politicians were not familiar with. A lot of financial planning had been done over the past several months in the absence of a sitting House of Commons. King's instincts pointed him towards seeking a fresh mandate from the electorate.

Constitutionally, he did not have to call an election until October 1940, but he decided a fresh majority would quell any cries from the Opposition benches. After updating the House of Commons on the details leading up to the signing of the BCATP, King said, "We are in the midst of the worst situation this world has ever known, and

I am afraid that the situation is going to get worse and worse. No one can say how long this war will last. Those who seem to be best informed tell us it is not going to be one year or two years; it may be three years; it may be longer than that. As respects the countries that may be drawn into the conflict, there appears to be a danger of the war spreading over vaster areas than were ever thought of before it began. So may I say that if we have to carry the grave responsibility of office in war and at a time of war such as the present, then we must be fortified by the voice of this country, expressed in no uncertain terms. We propose to leave it to the people of Canada to say whom they wish to carry on the Government of Canada in this period of world war. I move, Mr. Speaker, that the house do now adjourn."

The Governor General dissolved the 18th parliament later that day, January 25, 1940. With that, McKenzie King and his Liberal MPs hit the campaign trail in search of their fresh mandate. Canadians went to the polls on March 26, 1940. The Liberals got what they were seeking. Voters returned the McKenzie King Liberals to power with 179 seats, six more than in the 1935 election.

The Leader of the Opposition was incensed at the decision to head to the polls. In a fit of anger, Robert Manion compared McKenzie King to Hitler saying, "I am almost compelled to believe that he must have imbibed some of the spirit of Hitler when he made that well-publicized visit to the Fuehrer in Berlin a couple of years ago."

Manion's suggestion that the Prime Minister somehow shared the spirit of Hitler may have been partly accurate. In fact, McKenzie King's favorable impression of Adolf Hitler in 1937 raises a very sensitive question. Was there an undercurrent of anti-Semitism within the King Liberal government? The 1939 case of the ship MS St. Louis certainly suggested this to be the case.

THE MS ST. LOUIS DEBACLE

The MS St. Louis was a well-appointed, 17,000 tonne liner owned by the Hamburg-America Line. On May 13, 1939, the ship left Hamburg, Germany, bound for Cuba with 937 passengers aboard, most of them Jewish Germans who were trying to escape the Nazi threat. What the passengers were not expecting was a wall of anti-Semitism in Cuba. Upon arriving in Havana in early June, Cuban authorities ordered the ship to depart.

The ship's captain contacted U.S. authorities in Florida to negotiate a landing. The U.S. refused the captain's landing requests. A group of influential Jewish Canadians heard the story and telegraphed Prime Minister King, asking him to allow Canada to accept the ship and its passengers. King asked the External Affairs Department to consult with the Immigration Department. The whole effort then fell into a bureaucratic black hole. Days later, these departments advised King that the passengers were not eligible for admission to Canada. King accepted this explanation and decided not to use his power as Prime Minister to remedy the situation. King later recorded in his diary that the refugee situation was "much less our problem than that of the U.S. and Cuba."

The ship returned to Europe and distributed the passengers between the Netherlands Belgium, France, and Britain. When the war eventually broke out, many of these people were killed by the Nazis.

Does this undercurrent of anti-Semitism explain why the King government was moving so slow to express opposition to what Adolf Hitler was doing in Europe. The answer will likely never be known. However, in early 2025, a movement began in Canada to have McKenzie King's image removed from the Canadian $50 bill due to his perceived anti-Semitic beliefs.

CHAMBERLAIN OUT, CHURCHILL IN

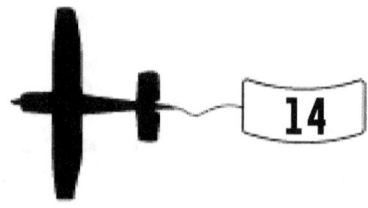

After having smashed through Poland in early October 1939, Hitler issued an order for the military to get ready to invade Luxembourg, Belgium, and Holland. However, by the end of 1939, Hitler had changed his mind several times. Luxembourg, Belgium, and Holland remined free, at least for the moment.

Joseph Stalin had been taken by surprise by the bold decision to advance German troops into Poland. He argued with Hitler and in the end Hitler signed an agreement with Russia stating that the joint aim of Germany and Russia would be to restore peace and order in Poland. No sooner was the ink dry on the agreement, than Stalin ordered his troops in Poland to restore peace. But peace was not what Stalin was after; he quickly laid claim to nearly half of Poland without barely firing a shot.

Despite having issued war declarations, Britain and France watched from the sidelines, the political aristocracy unwilling to create a repeat of the bloodbath that had been World War I. Hitler knew he had the upper hand; Britain and France were weak.

In the Atlantic ocean, German U-boats sunk nine British cargo ships, making a mockery of the British Navy. The German Navy's warship *Graf Spree* was plying the waters off Uruguay, sinking foreign ships as it went. The British Navy decided to end the mockery and strike back. In a skirmish off the coast of Uruguay, the *Graf Spee* was out-gunned and sunk by three British cruisers.

Undaunted by the loss of one of his warships, Hitler turned his focus to ensuring German steel mills had enough iron ore to make steel for building more ships. Germany was heavily reliant on Swedish iron ore to feed the German steel mills. During warm-weather months, the ore was shipped through Swedish waters. During the cold-weather months, Swedish waters often froze over. Ore shipments were then routed through Norwegian waters. In the British House of Commons, MP Winston Churchill argued that the British Navy be allowed to plant mines along the Norwegian shipping route used by Germany. Prime Minister Chamberlain refused to listen to the idea. Norway was neutral and Chamberlain wanted to keep it that way. Had Chamberlain agreed to lay the mines, World War II *might* have taken a very different course.

To protect the shipments of ore, Hitler unleashed the *Weser Exercise*. Five troop divisions were sent to take over each of Norway's main ports: Oslo, Stavanger, Bergen, Trondheim, and Narvik. He also sent two divisions towards Denmark. On April 9, 1940, leaders in Denmark capitulated without Germany firing a shot.

Although the five Norwegian ports were taken with only modest damage to German vessels, the King of Norway refused to surrender. In a radio broadcast, he urged the three million Norwegian citizens to stand up to the German invaders. This resistance drew a display of support from France and Britain. Within days, military troops arrived. However, they came poorly equipped and were greatly outnumbered by the Germans. In a fit of rage, Hitler ordered a campaign of destruction to be unleashed. One month later, the southern half of Norway was a smoldering mess. The British Navy, however, had come prepared and had laid waste to a significant portion of the German vessels it engaged with.

Hitler was not concerned with these sunken vessels; they too could be replaced. The German supply of iron ore was all he was concerned about - and it was secure. Hitler, who by now thought of himself as a military genius, turned his sights to conquering the Netherlands, Luxembourg, and Belgium.

The British RAF was also attacking German vessels from the air using its Vickers Wellington medium-range bombers. However, these larger planes were no match for the faster, more nimble, German Messerschmitt 109 fighter planes. Every flight mission resulted in British planes being destroyed by the Messerschmitt's which were equipped with machine guns; during May and June of 1940, 147 Wellington bombers were shot down.

The pressure on Prime Minister Chamberlain was crushing. He resigned as Prime Minister in May 1940, citing ill health. The Conservative Party elected former First Lord of the Admiralty and now back-bench MP from Epping, Winston Churchill, to become Prime Minister. Churchill immediately proceeded to also make himself the Defence Minister as well.

Hitler paid little attention to what was happening in the British parliament, focusing instead on his destructive advance through Europe. On May 10, 1940, Luxembourg gave up the fight. On May 15, the Netherlands admitted defeat after a devastating air raid on Rotterdam that left 1,000 people homeless and 80,000 dead. On May 28, Belgium capitulated.

The British RAF continued its attacks on the advancing Germans, but proved no match for the more-nimble planes of the German Luftwaffe. On May 12, 1940 alone, eleven Bristol Blenheim aircraft from a squadron of forty-two planes were shot down. Two days later, forty Fairey Battle planes from a squadron of seventy-one planes were blown out of the sky. In an effort to stem the losses, British air command decided to stop daylight bombing runs and focus instead on night assaults.

However, what the RAF commanders failed to realize was that aircrews did not have the navigational aids to properly locate targets in the dark, or under cloud cover. If factories on the ground turned off their lights at night, this further hampered the ability of British bombers to identify them as targets. In one spectacular failure in July 1940, a Bristol Blenheim bomber missed its dockyard target in Hamburg by three miles. Its load of bombs instead killed 19 German civilians. In an embarrassing event several weeks later, a bomber squadron headed for German targets in Holland encountered a severe lightning storm while enroute over the North Sea. The lightening interfered with the navigation instruments which caused the pilots to inadvertently turn the planes around. As the pilots unknowingly headed back towards Britain, they mistook the River Thames for the Rhine River and when they were certain they had identified their target they released their bombs. The bombs destroyed a British RAF fighter plane station. Luckily there were no casualties; just badly wounded egos.

Churchill knew Britain was in trouble. He was being pressured by Lord Halifax and other members of the aristocracy to give up; to sign a deal with Hitler. But Churchill had no plans to give in to Germany. He started to show his mettle and his oratory skills. He had a gift for motivating others through the use of carefully chosen and often graphic phrases. In the House of Commons in May 1940, he bluntly said, "If this island story of ours is to end at last, let it end when each one of us is choking in his own blood." In a speech to the students of Harrow School he said, " Never give in. Never, never, never. In nothing great or small, large or petty. Never give in except to convictions of honor and good sense. Never yield to force. Never yield to the apparently overwhelming might of the enemy."

"MR. CHURCHILL HAS REPEATEDLY DECLARED THAT
HE WANTS THE WAR. I AM FULLY AWARE THAT THE
CONTINUATION OF THE WAR WILL END IN THE DESTRUCTION
OF ONE OF US. MR. CHURCHILL MAY BELIEVE IT WILL
BE GERMANY. I KNOW IT WILL BE ENGLAND."

– Adolf Hitler

In addition to taking over Luxembourg, Netherlands, and Belgium, Hitler's troops had managed to surround over 300,000 British and French troops near the French port of Dunkirk. Churchill devised a rescue plan, *Operation Dynamo*, to get the troops and equipment out of Dunkirk. The plan made an appeal to British people who owned small boats to use their watercraft to rescue troops and equipment. In an overwhelming show of patriotism, an armada of small boats soon set out across the English Channel bound for Dunkirk.

What Churchill did not know was that two of Hitler's top commanders (General von Rundstedt and Luftwaffe commander Hermann Göring) were getting set to destroy the stranded troops at Dunkirk. Suddenly, Hitler changed his mind and ordered them to stand down. Why he had this change of heart is not known, but this sudden pivot provided *Operation Dynamo* the opportunity for the fleet of small craft to complete the rescue. Between May 26 and June 4, 1940, a total of 330,000 troops were evacuated and taken to safety. Churchill was relieved at the rescue of the troops. But the small boats could not handle the tanks and heavier pieces of artillery equipment. The loss of this equipment, left abandoned at Dunkirk, now left Britain more vulnerable than ever.

Winston Churchill remained desperate, although he did not show it. He needed help from other Commonwealth nations. Most of all, he needed help from American President Franklin Roosevelt; he needed the U.S. to join the war effort. Unfortunately for Churchill, the American people wanted nothing to do with another massive conflict. They had seen enough destruction and death in World War I.

Adolf Hitler did not care about what President Roosevelt was or was not thinking. He was focused on waging war and in late June, Hitler's troops rolled into France. While the politicians in Washington watched from afar, Churchill's diplomats were in advanced discussions with Canada regarding coming to the aid of Britain.

BCATP DETAILS

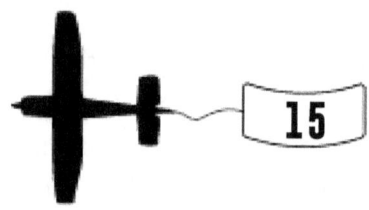

When the House of Commons resumed sitting on May 20, 1940, Prime Minister McKenzie King immediately came under Opposition attack over Canada having entered into the BCATP. He reminded the House of Commons that, "The British Commonwealth Air Training Plan is not an exclusively Canadian undertaking. As the name implies, it is a joint plan in which the four governments — those of the United Kingdom, Canada, Australia and New Zealand — are all concerned." Brushing off further criticism, he asked his Minister of National Defence for Air (Quebec MP Charles Power) to provide operational details on the BCATP.

The House of Commons soon learned that the Department of National Defence for Air would call up for service thousands of young men who had expressed a desire to join the air force effort. These trainees would first be sent to a Manning Depot, where over a five-week period they would learn to bathe, shave, shine boots, polish buttons, maintain their uniforms, and behave properly. They would receive two hours of physical education daily as well as instruction in marching, rifle drill, foot drill, and saluting. Following this initial training, a selection committee would then decide if an individual trainee would be selected for the Wireless Air Gunner stream, the Air Observer stream, or the Pilot Aircrew stream.

Wireless Air Gunner trainees would be sent to a wireless school where they would learn Morse Code and other communication techniques. In addition, they would learn aerial machine gunnery and bomb aiming.

Air Observers would be sent to air observer training for eight weeks, to a bombing and gunnery school for one month, and then to a navigation school for one month.

Pilot Aircrew candidates would be sent to an Initial Flight Training School for a four-week period. Over this period, they would study navigation, theory of flight, meteorology, duties of an officer, air force administration, algebra and trigonometry. They would be subjected to interviews with a psychiatrist, a four-hour-long physical examination, a session in a decompression chamber, and a session in a Link trainer (flight simulator). Following this initial training, they would be sent to an Elementary Flight Training School for a further 26 to 28 weeks where they would receive 50 hours of basic flying instruction on planes such as the De Havilland Tiger Moth. They would next receive 16 weeks of additional training which would include time at a Bombing and Gunnery School. (In Saskatchewan, there were two such schools: Dafoe No.5 and Mossbank No.2.)

Minister Power explained that construction of the aerodromes was the responsibility of the Department of Transport. Each of the 16 Initial Flight Training Schools would require approximately 108 planes. Each of the 26 Elementary Flight Training Schools would require twenty-seven planes. Each of the 10 Flight Observer Schools would require 24 planes. Each of the 10 Bombing and Gunnery Schools would require 75 planes. The two Air Navigation Schools would each require 48 planes.

For the fiscal year 1940-41, Minister Power said the government would be asking for approximately $124,000,000 in the budget. He further explained that Canada would be engaging in the manufacture of training aircraft to meet the needs of the various flight schools. Noorduyn Manufacturing (based in Montreal, Quebec) would complete building 56 Norsemen aircraft by September 30, 1941 and 210 Harvard aircraft by March 31, 1942. National Steel Car (Hamilton, Ontario) would complete building 116 Lysander aircraft by December 31, 1940. De Havilland (Toronto, Ontario) would complete building 554 Tiger Moths by September 30, 1941.

The direction and control of the BCATP would come under the oversight of a supervisory board that included Sir Gerald Campbell and Air Vice Commodore McKeen from Britain, Sir William Glasgow from Australia, and Group Captain Izitt from New Zealand. Canadian representatives would be the Minister of Transport (Mr. C.D. Howe), the Minister of Finance (Mr. Ralston), the Minister of National Defence (Mr. Rogers), the Air Vice-Marshal (Mr. Croil), and the Air Commodore (Mr. Johnston).

The supervisory board would meet every month to assess progress made. Minister Power noted that so far work was proceeding accurately and on plan. Aerodromes were being surveyed or developed, and some were already in operation. Many types of buildings were under construction with many already constructed. Every province of the Dominion would be represented in the BCATP.

MOSSBANK NO.2 BOMBING AND GUNNERY SCHOOL

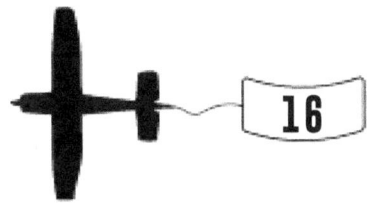

Early in 1940, for several days in a row, a plane was spotted in the air near Mossbank. It flew back and forth in a pattern. Nobody on the ground seemed to know what it was doing up there. In fact, it was a survey plane. The area around Mossbank was being considered as a possible location for one of the BCATP sites. The crew completing the aerial survey were attempting to identify an area of land up to one mile square with generally level topography that was also free of swamps, sloughs, hills, trees, and power lines. There had to be evidence of a source of gravel in the nearby area. There had to be ready access to a town or a village nearby that had basic amenities. Most importantly, if the site was to become a bombing and gunnery training facility, there had to be a lake nearby to drop bombs in.

The area near Mossbank ticked these boxes. The aerial survey identified an area just east of Mossbank that had suitable terrain for the construction of buildings plus 3,000 foot landing strips. The survey also showed that this area was in close proximity to Lake Johnston

(Old Wives Lake) and yet far enough away from the lake so that the airplanes on practice bombing runs could gain sufficient altitude before arriving over the lake. In addition, the surveyed area was close enough to Mossbank that personnel could enjoy social amenities when away from the training facility on furlough days.

The aerial survey crew prepared a report and sent it to the Department of Transport for further analysis. Transport officials then sent the survey data to the Aerodrome Development Committee for further assessment. Shortly after the Development Committee approved of the Mossbank location, a delegation from Canadian National Railways arrived in Mossbank. It would be their task to purchase enough land to accommodate the training facility.

After arriving in Mossbank, the railway delegation paid a quiet visit to several local landowners. The government agents explained that the federal government was interested in buying four quarters of land. (The term "buying" is not exactly accurate; the government would be expropriating four quarters using the legal tactic of *eminent domain*.) Old maps examined during the research for this manuscript confirm Mr. B.A. Schubert, Mr. T.B. Barnes, and Mr. Thomas Washbourn were the landowners approached by the government. The assessed value of land parcels in and around the quarters owned by these gentlemen ranged from $2,200 to $3,000. What exactly these gentlemen would have been paid by the government is lost in the mists of history.

Instead of relying on the Royal Canadian Engineers to move in and construct air training facilities, the RCAF created its own construction organization. Dick Collard, vice-president of Winnipeg-based Carter-Hall-Aldinger Construction, was recruited by the RCAF, given the rank of Wing Commander, and tasked with overseeing construction efforts on all sites across Canada that had been selected for BCATP facilities.

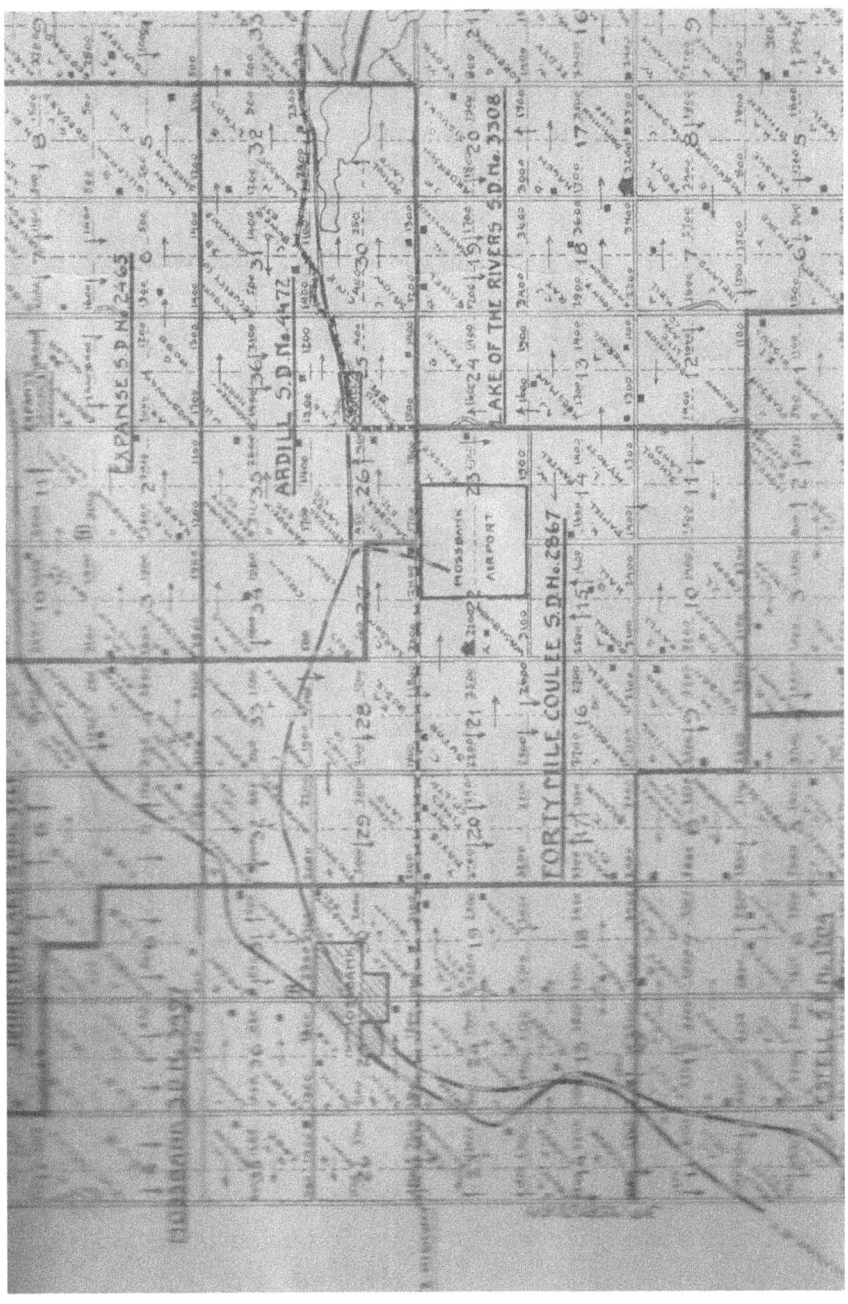

Map of RM 102 (circa 1940) Showing Location of "Mossbank Airport"

Eventually the government informed the public of the land acquisition. Residents of Mossbank and area who bought the July 25, 1940 edition of the *Lake Johnston Star* read that the Department of National Defence had selected a site some four miles southeast of the Town of Mossbank to establish a Bombing and Gunnery School. The newspaper article also noted that Defence officials had decided that up to 10 such facilities would be built across Canada to provide machine gun and bombing instruction to pilots, air observers, and air gunners.

On September 11, 1940, the Department of National Defence formally issued *Organization Order No. 60,* which stated that in order to provide adequate numbers of student airmen with bombing and gunnery skills, a facility to be called Mossbank No.2 Bombing and Gunnery School would be operational by October 28, 1940.

The operations plan called for Pilots, Air Observers, and Air Gunners to come to Mossbank No.2 Bombing and Gunnery School after having taken flight training at other training locations in Canada. Pilots coming to Mossbank would receive two weeks of machine gun training and bomb training and would then be deployed overseas. Air Observers would receive six weeks of intensive bombing instruction along with machine gun training and then sent on to an Air Navigation School for advanced training. Air Gunners would receive four weeks of training and then be sent to other training facilities in Canada for 24 weeks of Wireless Operator training.

By the time *Order No. 60* was issued, work at the Mossbank site had been underway for several months. The Poole Construction Company from Regina had been selected by Wing Commander Dick Collard to be the main contractor for the construction of the Mossbank facility.

Poole Construction - Moose Jaw

Poole Construction was founded by Ernest Poole in 1906 in the small community of Stoughton, Saskatchewan. The company soon established a reputation for quality construction of farm houses, barns, and stores. In 1910, the headquarters for the growing company moved to Rouleau, Saskatchewan. Poole's crew of about thirty carpenters began tackling larger, more demanding, projects such as town halls, schools, banks, and rinks throughout Saskatchewan and into Manitoba. The company headquarters moved to Moose Jaw in 1913 and then to Regina in 1914.

With such a solid reputation for quality work, it was no surprise that Poole Construction was selected as the general contractor in charge of building the Mossbank facility. The three sub-contractor companies that assisted Poole Construction were Sutherland and Berry Ltd. from Moose Jaw, Evans Gravel & Surfacing from Saskatoon, and water and sewer line specialist company R.B. McLeod Ltd. from Saskatoon. In addition, local Mossbank road building contractor Cal Sutor was engaged to assist with the construction efforts.

Cal Sutor (in the middle)

In 1940, getting construction materials to Mossbank was easy, thanks to the C.N.R. line which ran from Moose Jaw and through Spring Valley, Mitchellton, Ardill, and into Mossbank. However, getting supplies and materials from the rail siding to the project area was a challenge. One of the first tasks assigned to Cal Sutor was the construction of a rail spur line from the C.N.R. line into the project area. (A remnant of this spur line can be seen today close to the Hick Seeds seed cleaning operation which is located across Highway 2 from the site of the airbase.) After the successful completion of the spur line, Cal Sutor was then asked to assist with the building of streets and roads in and around the project area.

Conveyor loading gravel into dump truck

Sand and gravel for making concrete was sourced near the hamlet of Ardill. The exact location is no longer known. However, sand and gravel occurrences can still be found in the area near Ardill today.

Crane loading gravel

One of the first questions that Commander Collard was faced with was: what structural material should be used for building the hangars? With steel expected to be in short supply due to the war effort, the decision was made to use heavy wooden trusses for the hangars. Collard had his engineers come up with a standardized design for all the hangar buildings to be constructed across Canada. The design plans called for timber from British Columbia to be sawn into standard sizes and lengths. These component pieces would then be delivered by rail to each BCATP site. Workmen would follow standardized instructions and use steel brackets to bolt the wooden sections together to form trusses. Cranes would then lift the trusses into position. In total, six hangars were erected at the Mossbank site, each building measuring 224 feet by 160 feet.

Truss Assembly

Crane Erecting Trusses

Truss in Position

Two hangars being erected, one in the foreground, one in the background.

Completed truss structure for a hangar

Three months after hangar construction began, all six hangar buildings were substantially complete. The intended uses of the six hangars were:

- No. 1 Hangar: Daily aircraft inspection
- No.2 Hanger: Gunnery flight aircraft
- No. 3 Hanger: Drogue aircraft and Anson aircraft used for navigation training
- No. 4 Hanger: Bombing aircraft
- No. 5 Hanger: Maintenance and Repairs
- No. 6 Hanger: Engine shop.

Hangar buildings complete

By the time the hangars were completed, Poole Construction also had the Officer's Barracks substantially finished, the Officer's Mess partly built, the N.C.O. Barracks completed, the N.C.O. Mess done, and the Recreation Hall under way. Poole Construction hired local workers from the Mossbank area. Those with carpentry skills were paid 75 cents per hour while unskilled labourers were paid 40 cents per hour.

Coordinating the movement of construction supplies almost invariably intersected with government bureaucratic inefficiencies. One man in Ottawa had his thumb on the BCATP efforts across the country. If something was late getting to a site, he demanded to know why it was late, who was to blame, and when it would get there. His name was C.D. Howe, Minister of Supply. Throughout the construction of all BCATP sites, he worked tirelessly, slicing through government red tape and bureaucracy.

Planing Lumber for Constructing Buildings

Officers Mess Hall

Airmens Barracks Under Construction

Completed Barracks Buildings

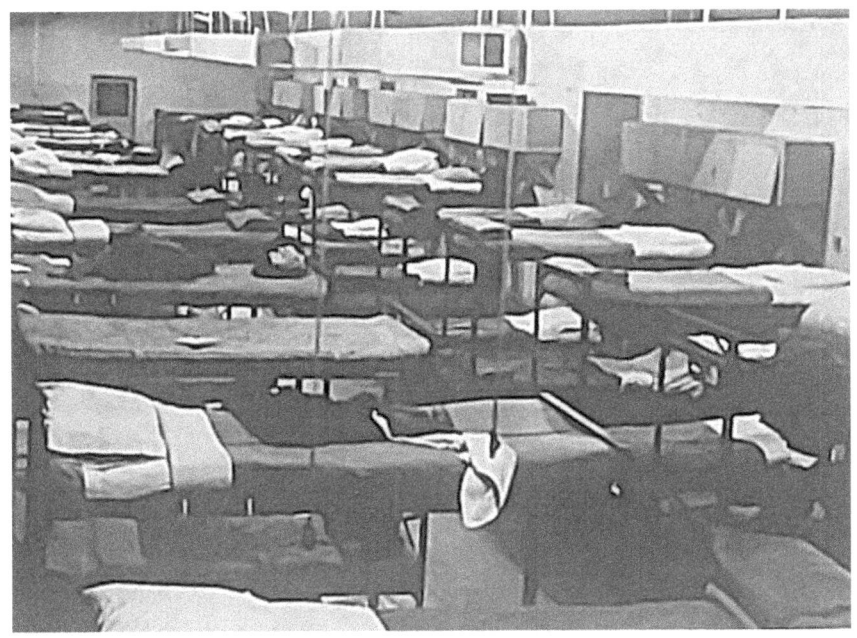

Inside A Barrack Building

Chapel

Mess Hall Under Construction

Control Tower Nearing Completion

Construction of the concrete struture for 25 yd firing range

Completed 25 Yard Firing Range

By late September, the trusses for the Drill Hall were up, the 34-bed Hospital building was begun, and the Headquarters building was nearly complete.

Drill Hall Under Construction

Then disaster struck. A workman left a torch unattended and the Headquarters building caught on fire. There were no fire extinguishers available and no supply of running water. The contractors could only watch in horror as the structure burned. However, with the October deadline for opening the Station looming, no time could be wasted. Poole Construction immediately embarked on building a new Headquarters structure.

Other facilities that were built between June and late September included: the Guard House, a Supply Depot, three vehicle garages, the airmen's Mess, a Canteen, the Civilian Quarters and Mess, a 25-yard firing range, a control tower, a Ground Instruction (G.I.S.) classroom, five bombing instruction classrooms, three machine gun training facilities, a sports field, tennis court, ball diamonds, an indoor sports pavilion, as well as a storage area for 20,000 gallons of fuel.

Burnt HQ Building

As buildings were being constructed, so too were three landing strips laid out in a triangular fashion; each strip being 3,450 feet long and 150 feet wide. The following images show the Hangar buildings in relation to the landing strips and an aerial view of the landing strips.

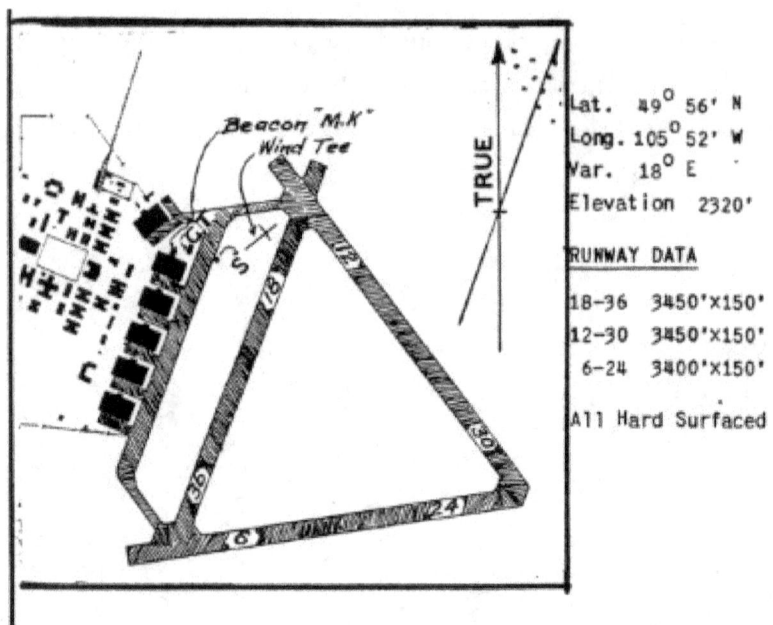

Three Landing Strips

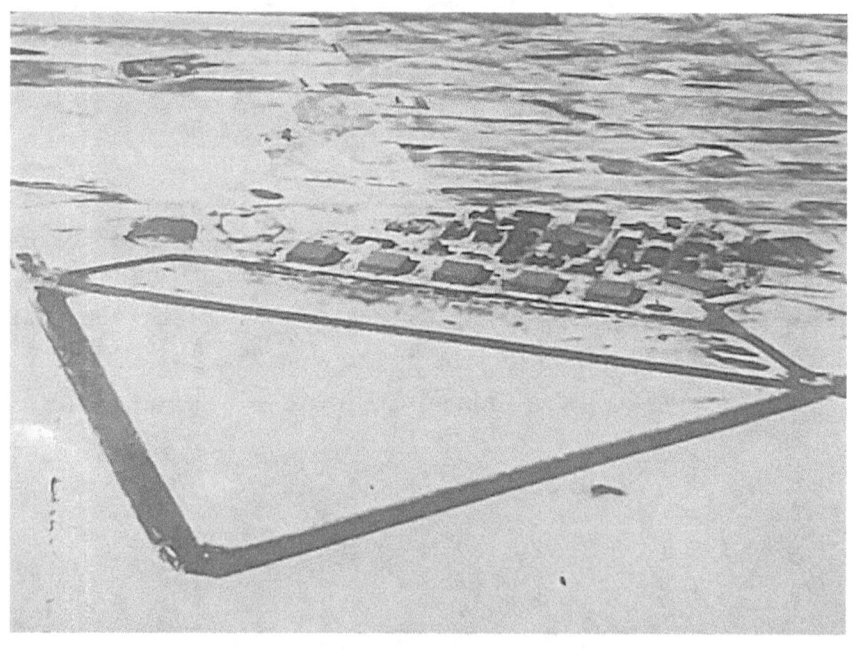

Aerial View

Running an efficient operation required more than just buildings. Over 10,000 individual supply items would eventually be stocked to make Mossbank #2 Bombing and Gunnery School run efficiently. These supply items ranged from fuel for airplanes to knives and forks for the mess hall. The task of managing the supply items was divided into groups. The Barrack Group handled crockery, beds, blankets, cleaning supplies. The Technical Group handled bomb-aiming equipment, radio equipment, tools, nuts and bolts, and aircraft parts. The Major Equipment Group handled airplanes, engines, and trucks. The Clothing Group handled all articles of clothing. The Publications and Stationary Group handled all stationery and government forms. The Gasoline Group handled oils, vehicle gasoline, and aviation fuel. The Shipping Group handled incoming and outgoing shipments of everything for all other Groups. The Salvage Group handled the many tons of spent cartridge casings accrued each month. Even scrap rubber from vehicle and aircraft tires was salvaged, collected, and sold.

Canteen

Recreation Hall

The first medical Doctor assigned to Mossbank No.2 Bombing and Gunnery School was Barrie Duncan. In a 1998 interview, he recalled the challenges of getting the airbase up and running. Initial attempts at drilling a water well near Ardill proved disappointing. A local water hauling operator was engaged to work practically around the clock to truck water from a well near Old Wives Lake to the air base so that personnel could use toilets and showers. Dr. Duncan and his wife lived in a trailer on the airbase. He was paid $7.50 a day as a Flight Lieutenant plus a living allowance of $1.70 a day. He recalls shopping in Mossbank where round steak sold for 25 cents a pound, T-bone steaks for 15 cents a pound and a 24-bottle flat pack of beer for $5.00.

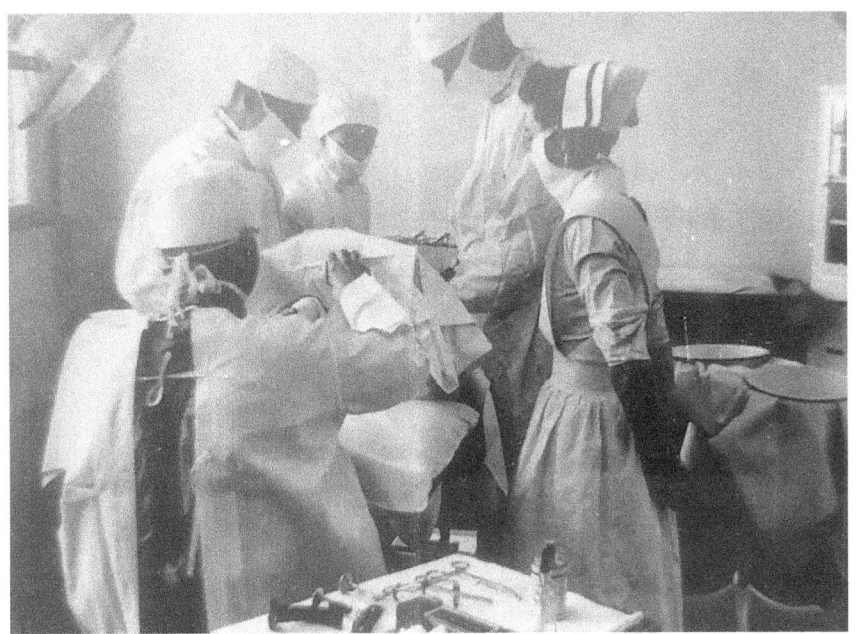

Hospital Operatng Room

F/LM.D.Williams,O.C.,N/SL.Carey,F/LR.B.Duncan,N/SM.Seaman,F/LChurch

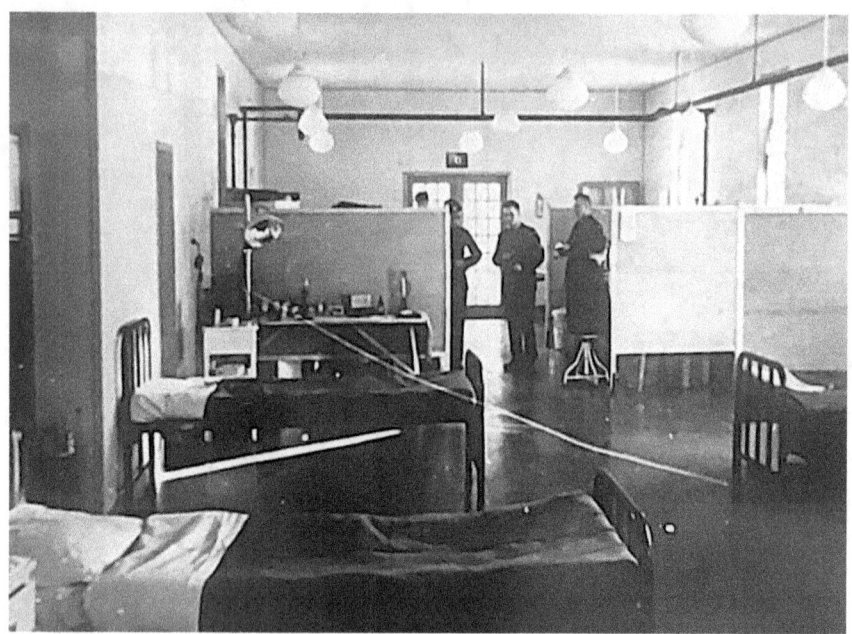

Hospital Beds

LONDON UNDER SIEGE

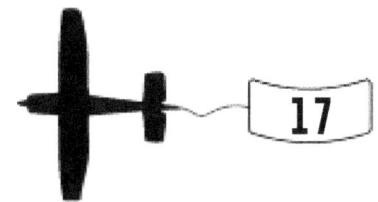

While BCATP construction was underway across Canada, the mood in Britain was turning grim. All that stood between Adolf Hitler and German control of Europe was the English Channel, and a stubborn Prime Minister Winston Churchill who was trying his damnedest to rally the British people.

Adolf Hitler was certain that Britain was in his grasp. On July 19, 1940, in an address to the members of the Reichstag he said, "The hour will come when one of us will break. And it will not be the Nazi Party." He went on to make it clear that it would be in the best interest of Britain to simply give up now rather than fight.

Upon being informed that Hitler had suggested that Britain should give up, Churchill's reply was one word: "No!" Adolf Hitler did not appreciate this negative answer. He decided to show Churchill what

Germany was capable of. On August 12, 1940, Germany launched Operation Eagle (*Adlerangriffe*) using 963 fighter planes, 998 bombers, and 316 dive-bombers. Adolf Hitler was certain that this attack would make Britain capitulate within a matter of days. Soon, Europe would be all his.

On August 15, 1940, the massive air assault hit British airfields, radar installations, and factories. Although the RAF lost four aircraft factories and sustained heavy damage to five airfields, it was ready for the German assault and laid a severe beating on the German planes. Nevertheless, Hitler persisted, ordering aerial assaults into British airspace, night after night, day after day, all focused on military targets.

And then came a fateful error in late August 1940. A squadron of German Junker 88 bombers became disoriented in heavy fog. One of the pilots thought he was near his military target on the outskirts of London when he ordered his bombardier to release the bombs. He was not on target at all. His bombs landed in the city of London.

The damage was light, but Prime Minister Churchill decided to show Germany what Britain was capable of. He ordered an aerial strike against a German city of similar size to London. The next evening, the RAF launched an assault on the city of Berlin. The British bombs hit their marks. Berlin took a pounding. This was the first time Berlin had ever been attacked in any war scenario. The people of Berlin were devastated and stunned. Their nerves were frayed and they were frightened. Hitler's war was now getting a bit too close to home. For the next two nights, the RAF flew similar missions on Berlin even going so far as to drop pamphlets with a printed message that reminded Berliners the war would last as long as Hitler stayed in power. Hitler was fuming mad. It was not supposed to unfold like this. Britain was supposed to fall. Instead, Operation Eagle saw the German Air Force lose twice as many planes as the British did.

In retaliation, Hitler then ordered a massive nighttime assault on British industrial targets along the River Thames. After eight solid hours of bombing, over 2,000 British citizens lay dead and thousands more were injured. Impressed with this assault, Hitler ordered a continuation of the carnage. After a month of successive similar night raids on London, Liverpool, Coventry, Southampton, Bristol, Plymouth, Manchester, Belfast, and Glasgow, nearly 60,000 British citizens had died.

With these casualty numbers inflating his ego, Hitler next ordered a daytime aerial assault on London. But Hitler was unaware of what had been going on behind the scenes in Britain. British code-breakers had learned how to decipher German communications. German Luftwaffe boss Göring was also completely unaware of this development. On September 15, 1940, code-breaking cryptographers at Bletchley Park realized something significant was about to happen. Deciphered code indicated that Germany was getting set to launch a major air offensive on Britain. Churchill made the decision to match the German move. All British air squadrons were ordered to take to the air; every plane, every pilot, every gunner.

Luftwaffe boss Göring was further not in tune with how well skilled the British had become with radar technology. From the moment the German planes became airborne, RAF technicians tracked their flight paths. Before the German planes made it across the English Channel, the RAF was ready. Damage to the German planes was substantial. A stunned Adolf Hitler flew into a rage at his Luftwaffe boss. How could Britain have known about the planned attack?

Hitler at this point realized that taking Britain would not be as easy as once thought. What he did not know, however, was that the British RAF pilots were weary and strained. The RAF had now lost one-quarter of its available pilots.

Over the next two months as German and British aircraft battled in the skies, Churchill walked the streets of London by day offering words of support to people who had lost everything in the bombing assaults. He became known for making a V-sign (V for Victory) with his index and middle finger. While his words and hand symbols helped to maintain morale, Churchill himself was feeling little optimism. He was painfully aware that Britain needed help and it needed it right now! He needed Canada to start sending pilots, navigators, and bomb aimers to join the fight.

MOSSBANK NO.2 OPENS

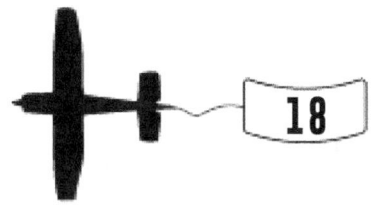

Group Captain J.A. Ashton, the first commanding officer of the Mossbank No.2 Bombing and Gunnery School, served from October 1940 to March 1942.

Born in England, Ashton came to Canada in 1911. The Canadian Air Force was formed in 1920 and Ashton joined it in 1921. His duties largely revolved around aerial surveying of Newfoundland and Hudson's Bay. When World War II began, he was placed in command of the Ottawa air station at Rockcliffe. He was later moved briefly to Jericho Bay, Vancouver before being assigned to Mossbank.

Ashton and a contingent of officers arrived by train in Mossbank between October 9 and 14, 1940. When Ashton arrived on site, construction of the facility was substantially complete. However, he soon learned that the facility he was to command had a special name. Building the Mossbank No.2 Bombing and Gunnery School in farm fields in the middle of nowhere had been a daunting task for the construction workers involved. Out of frustration someone had come up with the name *Calcutta Hole – The Last Post of Postings*.

Captain Ashton

Even though the facility buildings had been completed, several challenges still awaited Ashton, including securing a reliable supply of water. Without adequate water, cooking and laundry could not be done; toilets, sinks, and showers could not function; aircraft could not be kept clean; and the boiler system would not be able to provide heat to the various buildings.

Officers Arriving in Mossbank

Initially it was thought that drilling a well close by on Cal Sutor's farm would supply all the water the Mossbank facility would need. However, geography and underground geology are two critical factors when it comes to water in the Mossbank area. Wells in some locations will give water with elevated magnesium sulfate levels, while wells in other locations will provide reasonably decent drinking water. The water from the well drilled at Sutor's farm was elevated in magnesium sulfate (the main ingredient in Epsom salts) which acts to trigger diarrhea. Ashton's log book entry of October 10, 1940 makes this observation in a more delicate way:

October 10, 1940: *The consequences of normal consumption of this water are most distressing as it contains certain minerals which act as an acute purgative.*

Three water wells were then drilled in the coulee just west of the hamlet of Ardill. This time geology cooperated and these wells provided better quality water. Arrangements were also made with the C.N.R. station in Ardill to use some of their water as well.

Walking north through the pasture behind the Hick Seeds facility will bring one to the edge of a coulee. On the far side of the coulee, one can see the concrete structures of the water wells. Closer by, one can see the remnants of the storage reservoir for water pumped from the three wells. Water was trucked every day both from the reservoir and from the C.N.R. well to the airbase, a journey of nearly 3 miles. Records show that a volume of around 36,000 gallons was needed each and every day.

Finding space to feed the personnel posed a challenge for Ashton as the mess halls were not yet fully functional. Cal Sutor came to the rescue when he offered up a building south of the airbase to use as a temporary mess hall. This posed another challenge for Ashton. Contractors trenching water and sewer lines around the various buildings had not yet completed their work. The open trenches posed a safety hazard, especially after dark when personnel walked from Cal Sutor's mess facility back to their barracks.

In the absence of completed sewer lines, personnel had to use outhouses for relief. Hierarchy played a role even with outhouses. The sign on the door of the outhouse in one of the following photos reads "RCAF Personnel Only".

Organization Order No. 60 issued by the Department of National Defence clearly stated that Mossbank No.2 Bombing and Gunnery School would open on October 28, 1940. Despite the challenges in completing buildings, finding water, and finding space to feed the personnel, the October 28 deadline was met. On that very day, the first class of Air Observer trainees arrived. Six weeks later they received their graduation certificates and were dispatched for further training at other locations in Canada.

Trenches for Water and Sewer

Despite the on-time opening, some challenges remained for Ashton. In early November, the weather turned bitterly cold. Some of the barrack buildings still had no heat. The hangar buildings also had no heat. Office and classrooms were heated with kerosene heaters. Some of the printed classroom study material had not yet arrived. Ashton's logbook entry of November 6, 1940 diplomatically summed up the situation in a handful of words:

November 6, 1940: *Weather turning much colder. Generally, much distress is being experienced. A.O.s Course proceeding under difficulties.*

As snowfall began to accumulate, the loose dirt around the trenches became a slippery mess. The contractors responsible for completing buildings and finishing the water and sewer pipe installation were not always showing up for work. Finally, Ashton asserted his authority and gave a strict order to the various contractors to have heating and piping work completed within two weeks.

Outhouse RCAF Officers Only

Ashton next turned his attention to flight training. Many of the planes still did not have ammunition, magazines, and mounting brackets for their Browning machine guns. No sooner had he made progress on securing the needed gun supplies when labour issues arose. Someone at No. 4 Training Command in Calgary had made an arbitrary decision to pay the civilian contractors in Mossbank less than what they had been promised. The situation very nearly resulted in a mass walkout by the civilian contractors as Ashton's logbook details.

November 30, 1940: Civilian personnel, constituting the cooking and messing staffs, as well as firemen and other key positions are greatly upset at the action of No. 4 Training Command in directing that they be paid a lesser rate of pay than that stipulated at the time they were engaged by an Officer from Command Headquarters for employment on this Station. A $10.00 per month disparity exists between rates payable under this ruling and that which prevails at Moose Jaw and Regina. It is feared that the Civilian personnel will resign en-masse which would leave the Station in a situation which would be difficult to contend with. The Commanding Officer has drawn the matter to the attention of Command Headquarters, and action is expected to correct the discrimination, and remedy the injustice worked on the Civilians by this arbitrary departure from the agreements with them. It is extremely difficult to obtain Cooks, Clerks and certain other categories at the rates of pay which are stipulated for this Station.

It took four days, but Command Headquarters rectified the pay dispute and a walk-out was avoided. However, Ashton's challenges were not over yet.

GIS Building on Fire

A lingering safety issue facing the Mossbank facility was the potential for devastating fire. This potential again became reality in December, 1940 when part of the Ground Instructional School (G.I.S.) building caught fire. Personnel used hand-held chemical fire extinguishers for over two hours to fight the blaze. Ashton's logbook entry of December 11 references the lack of fire-fighting equipment:

December 11, 1940: *Had there been fire hose on the Station, or adequate fire-fighting equipment, the task would have been simplified and rendered more certain. A heavy gale might have endangered the whole Station,* *which is going to be in jeopardy until further chemicals arrive for the hand-extinguishers.*

Work immediately got underway to rebuild the burned portion of the G.I.S. building. As Christmas drew near, Command Headquarters in Calgary was expressing urgency to keep training students. Ashton decided that holiday time for personnel was not an option. Christmas Day was taken off, but then it was back to work. Ashton did however ensure that the tradition of officers acting as table waiters in the airmen's mess facility was upheld while everyone enjoyed a turkey dinner.

Officers serving airmen

By the end of 1940, Mossbank No.2 Bombing and Gunnery School had 52 officers, 536 airmen and 122 civilians on site. Commander Ashton had successfully managed the Station through its first few months of existence. His strict, unrelenting perseverance to project details would continue to guide the School which soon cast aside the negative references to the 'Calcutta Hole' and adopted the motto *Aim Well and Shoot Straight*. A crest followed, the design of which comprised a shield, a machine gun, a bomb, and the shield of the province of Saskatchewan.

No. 2 Bombing and Gunnery School Crest

CHALLENGES AND TRIUMPHS – 1941

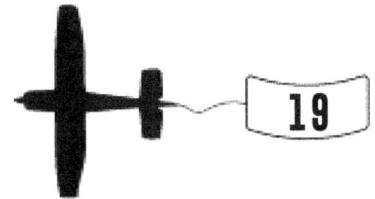

In early 1941, Britain was tired and weary. Hitler could easily have brought the country to its knees. But Adolf Hitler was not always a logical thinker. When under duress, he was prone to making rash decisions, often fueled by rage. He was easily distracted by competition to his superiority. He had grown alarmed that the Russians had advanced troops into the Baltic States and into the Balkan region as well. In Hitler's mind, Russian leader Josef Stalin was now a threat. In a classic fit of rage in December 1940, Hitler issued an order for Operation Barbarossa. Germany had to crush Russia. It was just that simple. The defeat of Britain was important, but Russia was more important at the moment.

The first stage of the operation called for the Balkans to be secured. What Hitler had overlooked was that Italian leader Mussolini also had similar plans to take territory in the Balkans, eastern Europe, and Greece. Mussolini, in his haste to conquer new territory, had overlooked the British Army. When the Italians arrived in Greece they were met head-on by the British Army. The Italian troops were routed. Undeterred by this news, Hitler ordered a mass invasion of Greece, Bulgaria, Yugoslavia, and Rumania. He was not the least bit afraid of the British Army. By April 1941, Britain had evacuated its troops from Greece. Greece capitulated as German tanks rolled into Athens. Bulgaria, Yugoslavia, and Rumania laid down their weapons too.

Instead of turning his attention back towards Britain, Hitler, now brimming with arrogance, turned his sights on Iraq and sent troops to Baghdad. This month-long logistical detour would prove costly, and indeed fatal. Towards the end of June, 1941 with Baghdad defeated, German troops began their march towards Russia. Hitler was sure that Russia would fall. He wanted Leningrad wiped from the face of the Earth. What he failed to grasp was that the harsh, unforgiving Russian winter was coming and his troops were marching into the jaws of it.

In Mossbank, the New Year brought with it a continuation of the water issues along with a host of new challenges. A blizzard in March of 1941 turned the ground at the facility into a wet, sloppy mess. Even the road to Moose Jaw, (not yet being an all-weather design) was impassable.

As the weather gradually turned warmer in May 1941, the muddy situation dried up. Work on the grounds of the facility then continued in earnest. Local contractor Cal Sutor was retained again, this time to improve the roads between buildings and also to construct an all-weather road from the facility buildings out to the main road. He was also tasked with levelling and generally improving the facility grounds so that the Dominion Experimental Station from Swift Current could seed the grounds to grass and plant shrubs and flowers in select locations. Cal Sutor delivered on his task of road improvement as Commander Ashton's logbook entry from September 16, 1941 expresses.

Muddy Mess Spring 1941

Water Everywhere Spring 1941

Receiving a Shipment of Supplies in the Mud

Stuck! Spring 1941

September 16, 1941: Our "all weather" roads are now complete, and we can claim to have a road system on the Station second to none in Canada. We can now look forward to "Rain without Mud".

WATER CHALLENGES

The water situation showed little sign of improvement. In early January, a watermain break caused the reservoir to lose its entire volume – 100,000 gallons. Records show that the daily water consumption was around 39,000 gallons. The wells in the Ardill coulee plus water from the Ardill C.N.R. well could barely keep up to what was needed each day.

Sometime around May 1941, the International Water Supply Company was hired to drill water wells that would provide adequate amounts of water to the Mossbank No.2 facility. The location selected for drilling these wells was very close to the shore of Lake Johnston. These wells are still in operation today and supply the Town of Mossbank with its water. The local Mossbank history book notes that Walter and Art Weiss worked with the drilling company taking water samples for testing.

To move the water from the wells to the airbase, a wooden waterline was laid. More accurately, the line was called a *stave-pipe culvert* and it had been made by the Canada Creosoting Company.

Visitors to Mossbank today who are interested in where this water line was laid need only speak to local farmer Henry Martens (JDH Organics) who will point out that the water line cut across the corner of one of the quarters of land that he owns. A remnant of the old water line is on display in the local Mossbank Museum.

Trenching in the Wooden Water Line

The Wooden Water Line

Sales Brochure for the Wooden Water Line

HEALTH ISSUES

The Dental Clinic which had opened in December 1940 under the command of Lieut. J.J. Schacter was put in the spotlight in early 1941. Dr. Schacter discovered that some personnel had developed Trench Mouth, clinically known as *ulcerative gingivitis*. The condition is a bacterial gum infection that can result in loss of teeth. Its causes include a failure to brush and floss, poor diet, and stress. In early 1941, dental floss had not yet been invented and penicillin to fight the infection was not yet being commercially produced. Severe health issues in the form of *encephalomyelitis*, an inflammation of the brain and spinal cord caused by bacterial infection, arose in Regina in the late Summer of 1941. Knowing that personnel on furlough often would go to Regina, Commander Ashton cancelled all leave passes and ordered personnel to remain on base.

OFF-SITE ACCOMMODATIONS

Not all airmen arriving in Mossbank were single. Some airmen arriving at Mossbank No.2, had their wives and young children with them. Commander Ashton was faced with the challenge of where to house these personnel. Again, it was Cal Sutor to the rescue. Ever the forward-thinking entrepreneur, he constructed a series of 12 wooden buildings in Mossbank and devised a plan to rent them out to airmen with families. These buildings earned the name "Sutorville." These structures were located where the Mossbank school is located today.

Sutorville Just After Completion

One of the Small Residences at Sutorville

Sutorville as seen from the air

An airman wishing to live away from the barracks at the Mossbank facility had to obtain a Permanent Pass document. The following image illustrates such a document issued to a Mr. M. Grudnitski. It allowed him to be absent from the airbase facility each weekday from 1700 hrs to 0730 hrs the next morning. He could be absent from the facility from 0001 hrs Saturday to 0730 hrs on Monday.

176 PERMANENT PASS

R.C.A.F. R. 174
100M-7-41 (476
H.Q. 1062-3-13

TATION #2 B-G School, Mossbank
NIT R.C.A.F. DUTY WATCH A.
No. R 77718. RANK Sgt
NAME Grudnitski M.

Has permission to be absent from his place of duty daily Monday to Friday from 1700 hrs. to 0730 hrs. and week-ends from 0001 hrs. Saturday to 0730 hrs. Mon (day) except when detailed for duty after normal working hours.
This pass must be produced on demand.
It is to be surrendered to Station Orderly Room on obtaining clearance on posting.

Issuing Authority

M Grudnitski
Signature of Bearer

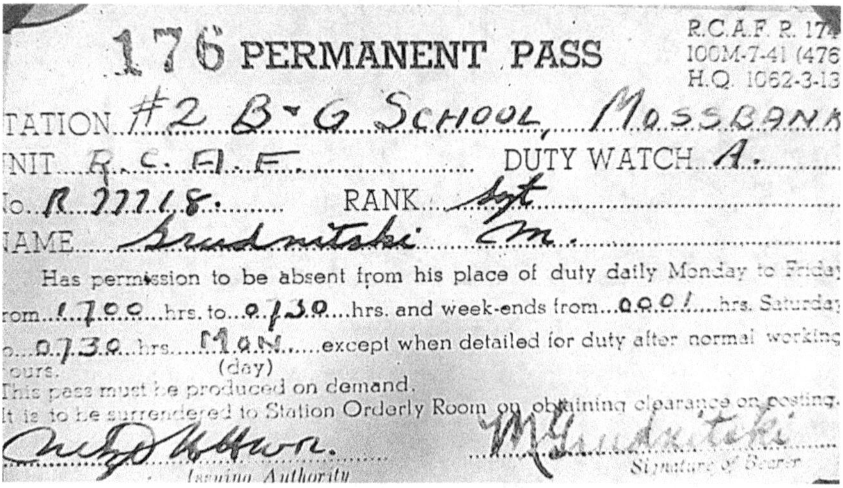

Permanent Pass

DISCIPLINE

Not all personnel were always at their best behaviour. Commander Ashton, who was a strict disciplinarian, met these behavioural challenges head-on as several of his logbook entries attest. His strict oversight extended to civilian contractors as well. A Sgt. Tylen flew his aircraft lower than allowed. He failed to document this occurrence in the Low Flying Logbook. This earned him a reduction in rank and 21 days detention. A civilian mess hall contractor from Moose Jaw was caught stealing coffee and tea. Commander Ashton referred this matter to the civilian law courts.

June 18, 1941: *R81327 Sgt. K.W. Tylen, No.2 Bombing and Gunnery School charged with (a) Low Flying (b) Failing to enter such low flying in the Low Flying Log Book.*

June 27, 1941: *The award of the Court Martial of Sgt. K.W. Tylen was published today, being found guilty of low flying and failing to report such low flying. Punishment awarded was reduction to AG2 and 21 days detention.*

July 18, 1941: *Before the Justices of Peace, Chaddock and Hensrud, at Mossbank, Sask., Mr. W. Mullen of Moose Jaw was fined $5.00 and assessed $4.50 costs and in default of payment 15 days in jail, on a charge of stealing two pounds of coffee and one pound of tea, the property of the RCAF whilst employed as a civilian messman at the civilian mess at this Station.*

EXPANDING THE MOSSBANK NO.2 FACILITY

As the war situation in Europe intensified, No. 4 Training Command in Calgary made the decision to expand the bomb aimer training program at the Mossbank No.2 facility.

Commander Ashton wasted no time in developing the necessary infrastructure on the shore of Lake Johnston. There were three floating targets situated on the Lake. The following image illustrates what they looked like.

Today, if one walks along the shore of Lake Johnston (Old Wives Lake), remnants of concrete foundations can be seen. These are the foundations of the bombing Observation Towers. A two-man Range

Crew situated in each tower would use a 'quadrant sight' to obtain a compass bearing of the position of the bomb's impact relative to the target. This data, along with time of bomb release, would be relayed back to the Plotting Office at base using Morse Code wireless transmission. Trigonometry calculations would then be used to determine the accuracy of the bombing attempt. Each two-man Range Crew would put in 10-hour days before being relieved by a night crew who would gather data from the night bombing runs.

Target in the Lake

Members of the Range Crew along with support staff lived full time along the shore of Lake Johnston. Three large tents with wooden floors housed officer quarters. A cookhouse and mess facility were created to provide meals. The tents were equipped with running water, lights, and a sewage system. To provide for after-hours recreation, there was a volleyball net, horse shoe pits, a slo-pitch ball diamond, and a canteen.

Range Crew in Front of Observation Tower at Lake Johnston

Cookhouse at Lake Johnston

One of the cooks managed to befriend a hawk. The following photo shows the cook with his feathered friend.

Cook with his pet hawk

The following image shows two of the personnel tents in the background. This area by Lake Johnston became known as *Tic-ville* due to the presence of small blood-sucking insects called ticks that lived in the grass.

Tents at Tic-ville

TRANSPORTATION

The challenge of getting personnel from the airbase facility to Mossbank and back again was met with the establishment of a bus service. Drivers included Frank Rose and his wife Winnie, Gordon Howlett, and Hal Brodin.

Winnie Rose Bus driver

SOCIAL ACTIVITY

The Town of Mossbank rose to meet the challenge of providing social activities for personnel. The local Masonic Lodge made their Lodge building in Mossbank available as a Hostess Club for wives of training airmen. The challenge of supplying a hostess each day was met by volunteers from The Red Cross Society, the Lake Johnston Chapter of the I.O.D.E. (Imperial Order Daughters of the Empire), and the Officer's and Airman's Wives Club.

The basement of the building, with seating capacity for 60 people, was converted into an Officer's Club which was open daily from 2:00 pm to 10:30 pm for the use by officers only.

Old Masonic Lodge Building

Sign for Hostess Club

Today, the old Masonic Lodge still stands in Mossbank (across the street from the Co-op gas station) but it has been converted into a private residence.

Good Times!

READING AND WRITING ACTIVITY

Commander Ashton arranged for the establishment of a reading facility as well as a postal outlet. The reading facility was sponsored by the Canadian Legion and had at any time a library of over 1,000 books and over 50,000 magazines. The books had been donated by local service groups in the greater Mossbank area. Popular novels of the day were Sigrid Undset's *Men, Women, and Places*, Bernard Newman's *Death to the Fifth Column*, and John Gunther's *Inside Latin America*. Airmen were encouraged to write to family to keep them apprised of their training accomplishments. Over 1000 sheets of writing paper and envelopes were given out each week along with about $35.00 worth of 5-cent stamps as personnel wrote and mailed letters.

Reading Materials

Writing Letters Home

WINTER

Training had to continue even during winter conditions. To ensure the landing strips were kept clear after a snowfall, Commander Ashton arranged for a snowplow to be at the ready.

Snowplow

Meanwhile, in Europe, the Russian winter arrived with a vengeance in early October 1941. The German troops were ill-prepared; no winter clothing, tank tracks freezing up, guns freezing up. The Russian troops who were prepared for winter, were fighting hard.

By late November, German troops, exhausted and approaching the breaking point, were within 30 miles of Moscow. Hitler, in his warm office back in Germany, was clueless. He had no concept of what his troops were experiencing. By early December with temperatures hovering around minus 35 Fahrenheit, the Germans could muster no more; the Russians had them surrounded. German hopes of taking

Russia were now crushed. Hitler, who prided himself on being a brilliant military strategist was in retreat; the German Army was broken.

In Mossbank, at the end of 1941, 57 Officers, 701 Airmen, 124 Trainees, and 107 civilians were hard at work. Commander Ashton had taken a newly-built greenfield site with mud, open trenches, and water issues and turned it into a well-disciplined, smoothly-functioning training facility.

BCATP EXTENSION

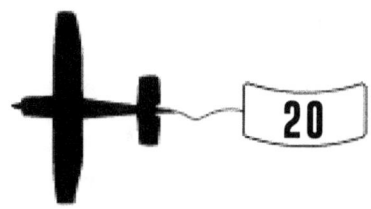

As 1942 dawned, Prime Minster Churchill was distressed that the bombing assaults in Germany had taken such a toll on British servicemen. Losses during 1940 and 1941 totaled nearly 4,000. Despite these losses, his only option was to continue the bombing assaults against German targets using airmen trained under the BCATP.

He issued a directive to unleash concentrated "area bombing" on civilian areas of German cities. This area strategy called for repeated waves of 200 or more Avro Lancaster bombers to each drop their 18,000 pound payloads of bombs on a particular German city until nothing was left but dust and dead people. By killing increased numbers of German civilians, he reasoned that German morale would suffer and an end to the war could be negotiated.

One of the first such missions in early March 1942 targeted the area around a truck factory near Paris that the Nazis were using to manufacture vehicles. A total of 235 bombers dropped their payloads on the area around the factory, severely crippling it. When the dust settled, 700 French civilians lay dead and 9,000 were homeless. Subsequent missions in April 1942 laid waste to the medieval German city of Lubeck and the ancient city of Rostock. On May 30, 1942 British air command decided to put on a show for the entire world to take note of. A total of 400 bombers utterly blasted the city of Cologne to bits. Pleased with this new strategy, in June 1942 Churchill pressed for the BCATP to be extended to 1945, well beyond its initial anticipated end date of March 1943.

The BCATP agreement signed in late 1939 came with a cost estimate of $600 million. The costs of extending the agreement from July 1, 1942, to March 31, 1945 were estimated at almost $1.5 billion dollars. Canada would assume fully $750 million of this amount. The governments of Australia and New Zealand would each bear the cost of having their respective airmen trained at facilities in Canada. The United Kingdom would assume the remaining costs in the form of an in-kind contribution of aircraft, engines, spare parts, technical equipment, bombs, ammunition and other supplies.

In Ottawa, a politically astute Prime Minister McKenzie King diverted focus from the cost figure and waxed prophetically to the House of Commons how the extended agreement reaffirmed and reinforced the determination commonwealth nations to help win the war. To cap off his comments with a positive spin he said the extended BCATP agreement emphasized the role of Canada, as "the airdrome of democracy."

BOMBS AWAY!

"WE SHALL EVER REMEMBER WITH GRATITUDE WHAT OUR
BRAVE YOUNG AIRMEN ARE SO VALIANTLY DOING TO DEFEND
THE SECURITY OF THEIR OWN CANADIAN HOMELAND AND
TO PRESERVE FREEDOM IN ALL PARTS OF THE WORLD."

– Prime Minister McKenzie King

"WE ARE NOW IN A POSITION, THANKS TO THIS TRAINING
PLAN CARRIED ON STEADFASTLY AND EFFICIENTLY AND WITH
DETERMINATION ALL OVER THE BRITISH EMPIRE, TO BE ABLE
TO SAY TO OUR FRIENDS AND FOES ALIKE, 'GIVE US THE
AIRCRAFT AND WE WILL, OUT OF THE AIR TRAINING PLAN, MAN
THEM AND FIGHT THEM AND ACHIEVE ULTIMATE VICTORY.'"

– Captain Harold Balfour
British Parliamentary Undersecretary for Air

Sign at the Entrance to Mossbank No.2

CAPTAIN HIGGINS ASSUMES COMMAND

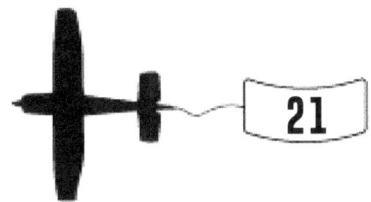

As 1942 dawned, America had now entered the war as a result of the Japanese bombing of Pearl Harbor in December 1941. As British Lancaster bombers laid waste to German cities, secrecy in the Canadian military became a priority. Commander Ashton was given a directive by Western Air Command to have civilian contractors take an Oath of Secrecy to ensure they did not spread details about what they saw or heard on base. Ashton's logbook entry of January 9, 1942 shows the concern over secrecy.

Jan 9, 1942: The importance of secrecy in the matter of postings overseas has been stressed to all personnel of the Station. The disclosure by personnel to friends or relatives of their posting overseas is strictly taboo. Information regarding the sailing dates of ships carrying RCAF personnel must not be divulged to friends or relatives. The taking of photographs at all RCAF Stations and areas adjacent is strictly taboo.

The urgency to hastily train airmen for overseas postings resulted in numerous accidents and fatalities. These occurrences were dealt with in a matter-of-fact way, which was the standard military approach in those days. The logbook entry of January 19, 1942 notes two fatalities and then immediately goes on to blur this reality with some flight-hour statistics.

January 19, 1942: Today, at approximately 1430 hrs, our Harvard No. 3797 crashed near Briercrest, Sask. Flight Lieutenant J.A. Peterson and Flying Officer C.F. Lawson were killed. This constitutes the first fatal crash since the Station opened nearly 15 months ago. A total of over 32,000 hours has been flown – averaging 16,000 hrs to a fatality. Prior to today the most serious flying hurt had been a sprained wrist.

A few weeks later, Commander Ashton received word that his time in Mossbank was up. He was being promoted and a new Commander was being sent to replace him. The logbook entry made by one of his subordinates reflects the respect that he was held in.

February 9, 1942: It has been a sad Station today, and a sadder Officer's Mess. We have learned that our Commanding Officer, Group Captain Ashton has been posted as Senior Staff Officer to Western Air Command. He has been C.O. of the Station since its opening. The glumness of the Mess was a silent testimony to the high regard in which he is held.

Ashton's replacement, Group Captain F.C. Higgins, arrived on March 5, 1942, to take over command duties. He would remain in charge until October 1942.

In 1942, Mossbank No.2 decided it needed a mascot. The job was given to LAC "Stubby." The name Stubby was unfortunately earned in an encounter with a grass cutting mower which severed his right paw as the following photo shows. Stubby served with distinction until 1944 when he took his retirement as mascot and was promoted to a more leisurely lifestyle. He was replaced by a 200-pound, purebred St. Bernard named Rex.

Captain F.C. Higgins

LAC Stubby

WE SERVE THAT MEN MAY FLY

In 1942, the roster at the Mossbank facility came to include a new category of military personnel – airwomen. In 1941, the groundwork for employing women was laid when the federal government took over Old Havergal College in Toronto and created a training school known as the C.W.A.A.F. (the Canadian Women's Auxiliary Air Force). In October 1941, 150 young women from various parts of Canada reported to Old Havergal College in Toronto to begin training as airwomen. The month-long training program was conducted by four female instructors: two from Britain and two from the United States.

Women in the RCAF compiling Aircraft Maintenance Records

At the end of the training program, the new C.W.A.A.F. inductees were dispatched to their new locations. In 1942, the C.W.W.A.F. was renamed the RCAF (W.D.) to denote Women's Division. Very quickly, RCAF (W.D.) women proved they could perform tasks ranging from aircraft maintenance and parachute rigging, to photography to, as well if not better than men. In all, there were 52 trades that RCAF (W.D.) women could engage in.

On May 17, 1942 a contingent of 60 women arrived in Mossbank. They were assigned to positions in 22 of the 52 designated RCAF trades. To celebrate their arrival, on Saturday May 30, 1942, a dance for airmen and airwomen was held in the Recreation Hall. Music was provided by the Mazenod Major Ramblers from Mazenod, Saskatchewan.

As intriguing as women working in trades sounds, there was considerable inequity. On average, airwomen made $30 per month, which was about two-thirds of what their male counterparts made for similar work. This likely explains why by July 1942, the number of women enlisting in the W.D. program had dropped off markedly.

In late May, *Regina Leader Post* writer Kay Kritzwiser was flown to Mossbank to learn more about airwomen. She was toured through the Mossbank facilities by Barbara Rook. Ms. Kritzwiser shared her observations in an article titled *Responsible Jobs Held By Airwomen*. Here are some excerpts taken from her article:

I soon met Barbara Rooke, who arrived at Mossbank two weeks ago to make preparations for the first section of airwomen. She is a thoroughly attractive person. Her eyes are blue and she does her dark hair in that smooth halo-roll and there's nothing "battle-axe" about her, but you can feel she can be tactfully official if need be.

"There were 66 girls that arrived last week in the first draft," she pointed out. "That number should go up to 138. This means there will be 138 airwomen filling jobs such as dental and hospital assistants, drivers, parachute riggers, magazine loaders, clerks, messwomen, and cooks."

In the airwomen's quarters, it was clean sheet day and all the mattresses were stripped of their linen. The mattresses are soft and well-built; I poked one to see. No roughing it here, by any means. The beds get an issue of clean linen once a week. They are double-decker affairs and said to be extremely comfortable. It was mid-morning and the place was neat like a pin. There is linoleum over all the floors to keep them shining and the girl's lockers against the walls are painted white.

Next to the girl's living quarters are the utility rooms. There are five showers, two tubs, and several rows of wash basins with mirrors above them. It's an attractive place, painted pale green – a fine chummy place where the girls set their hair, and smear gobs of cold cream on their faces and bend into the mirrors to tweak out eyebrows.

E. Reed, Women's Division C.O.

There is a large, airy laundry room for the girls, with drying racks, an ironing board, and an iron. The girls have their heavy laundry done for them, but the shirts and the stockings and the bits of undies hanging on the lines - no girl ever trusts to a laundry to do these for her.

The airwomen's recreation hall isn't finished yet, but "when it is it will have lounges and deep chairs and those little knee-high tables, and a piano – we hope," said Rooke. There is a canteen attached, a dry canteen – no wet canteen for airwomen, and that's quite understandable. The canteen will provide snacks like soup and sandwiches, cookies, and soft drinks.

Up to a short time ago the cement floors of the maintenance hangars had echoed to nothing but the clack-clack of masculine heels. Today it was different. The first airwoman was at work in one of them, working as an equipment assistant, a smear of grease on her nose. There will be other women to join her as equipment assistants in the hangars as others arrive at the station.

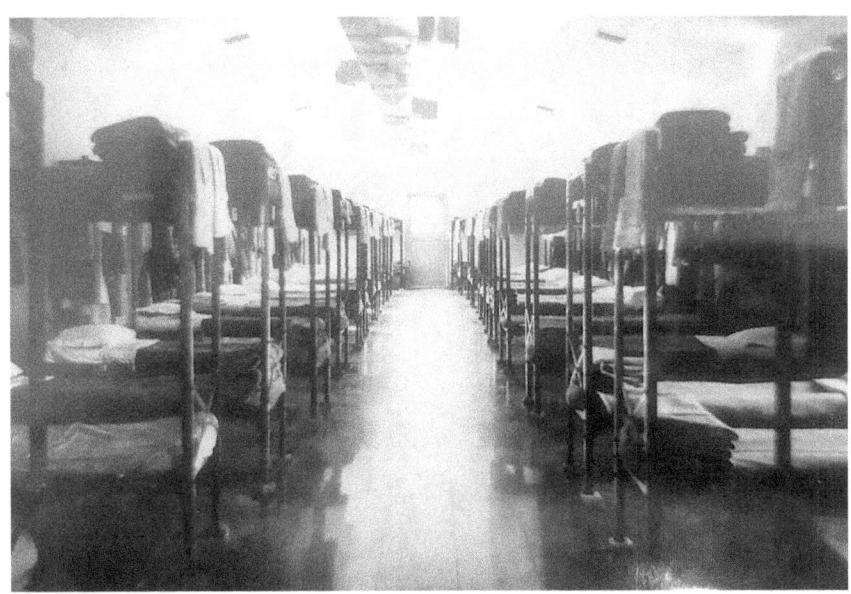

Beds in Womens Division Barrack

Up in the control tower there was an attractive AW2 from Winnipeg who represents one of the new trades for airwomen. Right now, she was familiarizing herself with the wireless. Her job will be to keep in touch with the bombing planes as they come and go around the station.

Airwomen have been put in charge of clothing stores now too, helping to supply the clothing needs of the airmen as well as the airwomen. Corporal H.M. Bidlake of Vancouver, one of the airwomen in clothing stores looked up from her list making to say she hadn't come across any prima donnas yet among the girls as far as clothing went. Girls have fairly regulation figures and there is very little trouble with fittings – nothing that can't be remedied easily at the station's tailor shop.

In the months immediately following the *Leader Post* article, the Mossbank No.2 facility had 114 airwomen on the roster.

Sewing Room

All work and no play is never a good thing, even for women in the military. Some airwomen found off-hours enjoyment in the sewing room.

Others discovered that the nearby hamlet of Ardill had a Hotel. Quite often groups of airwomen would make their way to the Ardill Hotel for a beverage as the following picture shows.

Visting the Ardill Hotel (L to R: Goodwin, Bodkin, Brough, Burns, Kerr)

As intriguing as the *Regina Leader Post* article was, serving in the military was not easy for some airwomen as the following entry in Captain Higgins' logbook attests:

September 10, 1942: Regrettable occurrence in the death by self-administered poison today of A/Sgt. (Unpaid) Seymour, H.W. Sgt. Seymour was an excellent type of Airwoman and had been recommended for a Commission some months ago and later sent on a Course. During the Course she apparently suffered a mental breakdown which affected her permanently. At the time she was returned to this Unit she was to all appearances very much improved and it was considered that back to her normal routine here might clear it up. However, a few days later she showed signs of a setback, was admitted to Hospital, and took the step she did with fatal result.

MOSSBANK NO.2 TRAINING

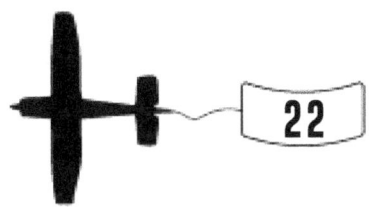

Air Observer trainees arriving at Mossbank No.2 Bombing and Gunnery School received training over 18 weeks that included: airframe and engine study, aircraft recognition, aerial gunnery, Morse Code signals, navigation, photography, reconnaissance, theory of bombing, Link Trainer practice, and insights into the latest warfare developments of enemy countries. The training was not easy with about 16% of students failing to pass.

AERIAL GUNNERY

Aerial gunnery skills were developed by having student airmen in a Bolingbroke aircraft shoot at a drogue that trailed behind a Lysander aircraft flying parallel to them.

A drogue resembled a large cylindrical-shaped kite, approximately 30 feet long and about 3 feet diameter. Construction material was a light-weight fabric, likely a blend of cotton and silk. Once airborne, the drogue operator in the Lysander would release a 300 foot cable. Attached to the end of the cable was the drogue.

The bullets used by the student airmen were loaded with a colored dye. The student in the turret of the Bolingbroke aircraft could look through the glass windows of his turret and see the nearby Lysander aircraft towing the drogue. His goal was to ensure as much ammunition as possible hit the drogue target. Back on the ground, the drogue analysis team would count the number of colour-stained bullet holes. The student would then be taken aloft again to repeat the shooting exercise. Student airmen were constantly reminded that shooting accurately from a turret would be a matter of life and death once overseas in a real war situation.

Herb Arndt, an elderly gentleman now living in Medicine Hat, Alberta has vivid memories of the drogues. Sometimes a technical failure would result in the drogue separating from its cable and falling to the ground. As a young lad he remembers occasions where he would find drogues in the farm fields near his family's farm. Returning the drogue to the Mossbank facility would earn him a $2 finder's fee (equivalent to almost $25 in today's inflation adjusted currency).

AIRCRAFT RECOGNITION

Aircraft recognition training was conducted with the student positioned behind a hemisphere-shaped tent designed to simulate an airplane turret. A small model aircraft mounted on a moveable assembly would appear in front of the hemispheric turret assembly. The student was equipped with a mock machine gun. He would have to quickly look at the model aircraft appearing in front of him and in a split-second would have to decide if it was friend or foe. If he deemed it to be an enemy aircraft, he would announce out loud the type of aircraft he was shooting at. He would then open fire and the mock gun would send an electrical signal to a ticker tape recording device. If the image depicted an Allied aircraft he would not open fire. Later analysis of the ticker tape would determine how many shots he had made.

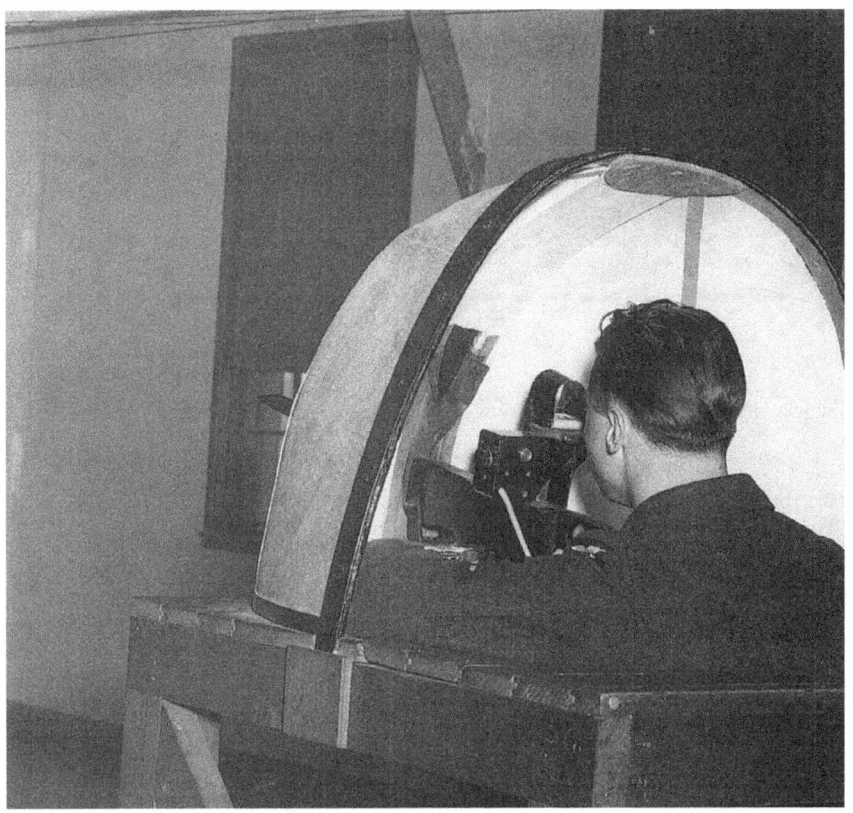

Aircraft Recognition Training

The following image is taken from the April, 1944 issue of *Target* – the periodic publication produced for those serving at the Mossbank facility. This visual recognition quiz challenges the reader to determine the difference between the silhouette images of two planes.

Target April 1944

The answer to the quiz is – fire at #2. It is a German Dornier twin-engine bombing aircraft. Aircraft #1 is a friendly Douglas C-54 transport plane.

TURRET MANIPULATION AND FIRING

An air observer had to develop turret manipulation skills. A student airman would be placed in a turret that had been taken from an actual aircraft. He would practice rotating the turret and handling the turret's weaponry. At the 200-yard range located at Lake Johnston, students could fire tracer bullets from machine guns mounted on their turret training assembly. Firing was often done in various weather conditions to give the trainee a sense of what real combat situations would be like.

Shorter distance Shooting Ranges were also used extensively by student airmen. At the 25-yard range, students practiced elementary firearm skills. To further improve trigger finger to eye coordination, students often made use of the skeet shooting range.

Airmen Practicing Turret Skills

LINK TRAINER

The Link Trainer was designed and patented in 1931 by American inventor Ed Link whose family owned the Link Piano and Organ Company.

This flight-simulating trainer was built using the same type of air bellows that were found in an organ. Air pumps built into the analog circuitry operated the instrumentation on the trainer. The bellows ensured a fluid response to the student's movement of controls which gave the student the feeling of flying a real aircraft. The student airman sitting in the trainer could move the controls and make the entire device bank right, bank left, climb, or dive. Students who spent time on a Link Trainer quickly became proficient at instrument flying.

During World War II, Ed Link sold over 10,000 of his Link units to militaries around the world. The Link Trainer went on to become the genesis of the modern day aircraft simulator used by airlines the world over.

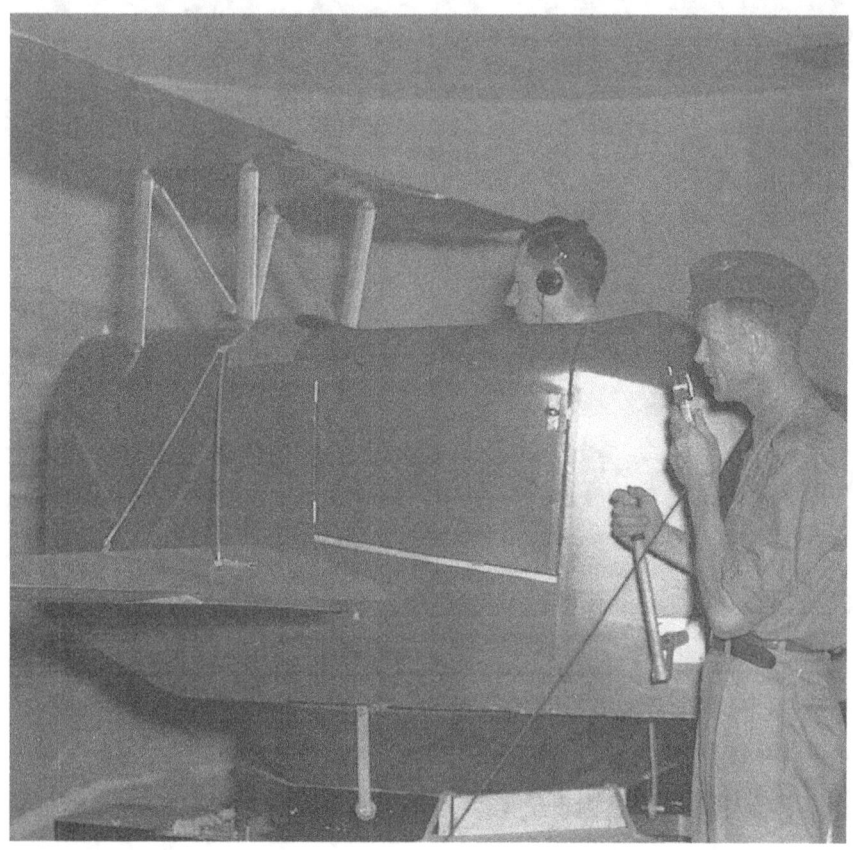

Student airman in the Link Trainer

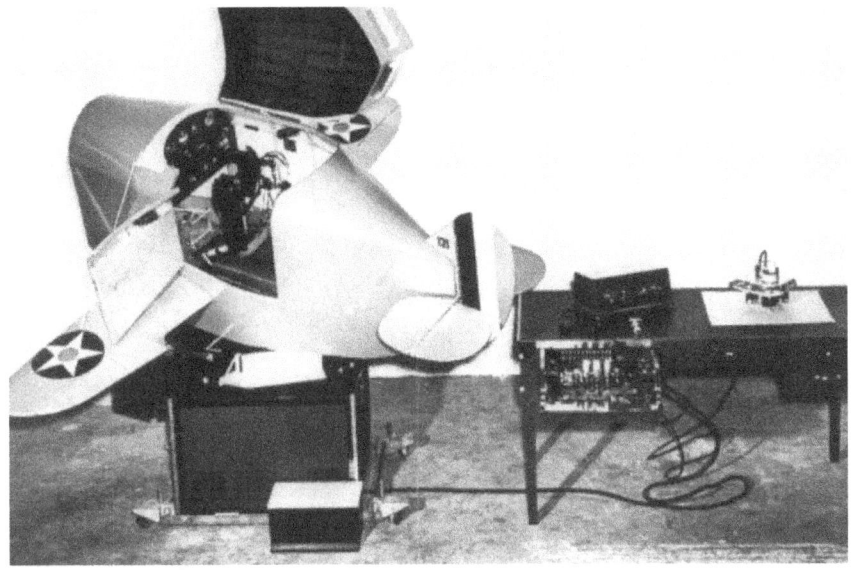

Link Trainer

AIR GUNNER WIRELESS OPERATOR

Air Gunner Wireless Operator training was a separate 20-week training program at Mossbank No.2 Bombing and Gunnery School.

As the name implies, Air Gunner Wireless Operators were primarily responsible for aerial gunnery. But they were also responsible for Morse Code wireless communication at a proficiency of at least 18 words per minute to communicate changes in wind speed and weather back to the control tower. They would also have to maintain communication with other aircraft flying in the area.

They also functioned in back-up roles including assisting in bomb aiming, assisting with casualties on board, manning a gun turret, and assisting with navigation to help the pilot get the aircraft back to base in the event the navigator was wounded.

Certificates of Qualification

(To be filled in as appropriate)

1. This is to certify that NZ 425285 LAC NEWEY G.
.has qualified as W. Op.
with effect from OCT 1 1943 Sgd. W. Fisher
Date OCT 1 1943
FOR C.O. NO. 3 W Unit RSS SCHOOL,
WINNIPEG, MAN.

2. This is to certify that NZ 425285 Sgt NEWEY G
has qualified as AIR GUNNER W. OP.
with effect from NOV 2 2 1943 Sgd.
Date NOV 2 2 1943 Unit
CHIEF INSTRUCTOR, No. 2 BOMBING AND
GUNNERY SCHOOL, R.C.A.F. MOSSBANK, SASK.

3. This is to certify that

Air Gunner/Wireless Operator certificate issued to a Sgt. Newey

Upon completion of training, the student would receive a graduation certificate. The above image shows that a student by the name of G. Newey qualified as a Wireless Operator in Winnipeg, Manitoba and then as an Air Gunner Wireless Operator in Mossbank.

One of the Air Gunner classes at graduation

WIRELESS SIGNALING

Morse Code, originally invented in the 1830s as a way of sending messages by electrical telegraphy along telegraph wires, is comprised of dots and longer dashes to represent the letters of the alphabet. This method of communicating was particularly popular with railways where a Station Master could send a message to another Station along the line.

Replica of a Wireless Transmitter (owned by Donny Smith)

Although there are no telegraph wires in the skies, thanks to the technical genius of Italian inventor Guglielmo Marconi it was possible to send Morse Code messages wirelessly. Marconi did not receive formal school education; his parents, who were of financial means, hired private tutors to educate him. When Marconi was 17 years old, he was introduced to the work of Scottish scientist James Clerk Maxwell and German scientist Heinrich Hertz. The research of both these gentleman focused on what they were sure was an electromagnetic field that surrounded planet Earth. By the time Marconi was 20, he had created a spark-producing transmitter and a crude receiver. He demonstrated that he could transmit Morse Code a distance of half a mile. With modifications to transmitter, receiver, and antennas, much longer distances were soon realized. Thanks to Marconi's work, planes could send Morse Code messages that would be picked up by receivers up to 100 miles away.

Mossbank resident Donny Smith's father was born in Fort William, Ontario (now Thunder Bay). After serving in World War I, he took employment with C.N. Rail and in the 1920s was transferred to Lake Lenore, Saskatchewan (about 140 kms northeast of Saskatoon).

Mossbank CNR Station 1943

In the late 1930s, Mr. Smith and his family were transferred to Mossbank, Saskatchewan where Mr. Smith became the C.N.R. Station Agent. The family lived in the Mossbank C.N.R. station building and Donny Smith has memories of hearing the tap, tap, tap of Morse

Code messages on the receiver in the train station practically around the clock. Many of those messages were being sent by aircraft in the air around Mossbank.

BOMB AIMER TRAINING

Bomb Aimer training was a 12-week process. The first two weeks were devoted to classroom instruction. Mossbank No.2 had four synthetic training devices (called *Air Ministry Bombing Teachers*, or A.M.B.T.s) that resembled an aircraft cockpit. Each of the four was slightly different as they were modelled on the different types of aircraft students would encounter when sent overseas.

Plotting Office

A picture projector positioned above the training apparatus projected a film image downwards. The student sitting in the training device only had to glance down to see what looked like ground scenery moving past him. This gave the simulated feel of motion. The student could then select his target from the image he saw beneath him, do his calculations, and drop bombs.

Towards the end of the second week, students were introduced to the layout of the Avro Anson bomb-carrying aircraft, the bombardier's cockpit, and the various switches and controls.

Finally, it would be time for practical bomb-aiming training. Groups of student airmen were ordered to report to the Plotting Office at 07:25 hrs on "fly day". They would select their flying clothing from the Check Room and proceed to the Crew Room.

Pairs of students would hear their names called over the loudspeaker system. They would select their parachutes, their electrical telecommunication sets, and report to the pilots who would be flying the bomber aircraft. The students and pilots then would make their way to the Briefing Room where they would receive last-minute mission instructions from the Briefing Officer.

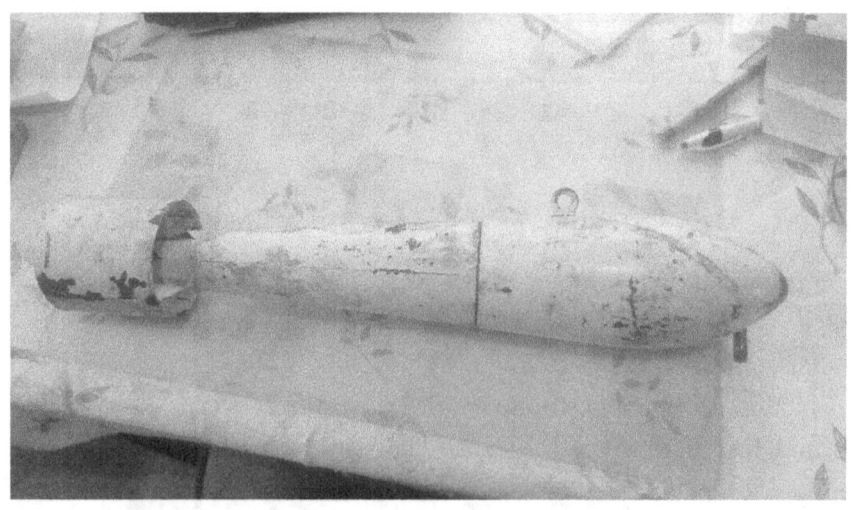

Bomb Casing (part of the private collection of Donny Smith)

The students and pilots would next proceed to the aircraft situated outside on the tarmac where they would inspect the 11-pound bombs that had been loaded into place by armourers.

The bomb casings were made of steel. The heavier, cast-iron nosepiece of the bomb was connected to a firing pin. Inside the nose was a small amount of percussion charge material. In the tail section of a bomb was a glass vial containing titanium tetrachloride, a volatile liquid chemical. When the bomb would hit either the target or the surrounding water, the impact would drive the firing pin into the percussion firing material. The percussion would shatter the glass vial containing the titanium tetrachloride chemical which would react violently once exposed to air or water and produce a puff of smoke. The azimuth location of the puff of smoke would be measured by the Range Crew in the bombing observation towers.

One of the students would crawl into the bombardier cockpit located in the nose of the aircraft. The other student and pilots would take their place in the main cockpit area. The student in the bombardier cockpit would next check all switches, sights, and communications devices. The aircraft would taxi to the designated runway, take off, and climb to the height authorized by the Briefing Officer.

The airplane would make its way several miles northwest of the airbase to Lake Johnston where the target site on the lake could be seen by the student positioned in the nose of the aircraft. Using the mathematics learned in the classroom, the student would take into account factors such as altitude, wind direction and speed, and ground speed. He would release his bombs accordingly, sending them on their way towards the target which was mounted on an empty, floating 45-gallon oil drum in the lake. After several such runs, the student in the nose of the plane would then switch places with the second student and a series of new passes would be flown over Lake Johnston.

Finally, back on the ground students and pilots would report to the Interrogation Room for questioning and debriefing. Once thoroughly questioned as to how the bombing run had proceeded, the students would report to the Plotting Office where they would be presented with the timing and accuracy data gathered by the Range Crew.

This data in hand, the students would report to the Analysis Room where an in-depth study of the data would be conducted. The students would then report to the Crew Room to repeat the process all over again.

The following image shows a group of airmen at the Mossbank train station. Their training in Mossbank being complete, they are on their way to another location for additional training.

On to Next Assignment

ACTIVE, FIT AND WELL FED

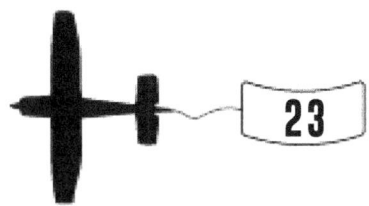

The RCAF recognized the importance of having the airmen and airwomen stay physically fit. No effort was spared to provide opportunities for fitness. In fact, five hours per week of physical activity was mandatory.

At a typical fitness session, running and calisthenics were used to get the body warmed up. What followed were games such as basketball, soccer, badminton, and floor hockey. Fitness training also included obstacle course work and gymnastics.

In late 1942, a swimming pool was built. Airmen trainees were expected to become competent swimmers; those who displayed weak abilities in the pool were given intense instruction until their skills improved. A trainee who could not become a strong swimmer would not become a pilot, navigator, or bomber. The rationale behind swimming competence was that a strong swimmer would be able to save not only himself but the lives of fellow airmen in the event that a plane was downed over water. To more fully utilize the pool, a Water Polo League was created in March of 1943.

Pool

The following entries from the Commander's logbook offer further insight into the physical fitness activities:

May 1, 1941: A Boxing Tournament was held in the Drill Hall at this Station this evening between (RAF) Moose Jaw and our School. There were five bouts and we won four of them. The tournament was well attended. The Station orchestra provided music between bouts and during the intermission.

Boxing

Not all physical activity was confined to the Station. Under supervision of an Officer, personnel were sometimes allowed to venture away from the Mossbank facility. The area mentioned in the following logbook entry refers to a long, narrow valley that was formed after the last ice age by glacial meltwaters. The north end of the valley opens up to Lake Johnston and south-east opens up to Willow Bunch Lake located southeast of Assiniboia. The logbook entry refers to Menchenko's Dam. This is most certainly a spelling error. It should be "Mowchenko's Dam". Various members of the Mowchenko family own farmland along this river valley to this day.

July 17, 1941: An "Old Swimming Hole" has been discovered some 14 miles southeast by road and is known as Menchenko's Dam. It is an old river bed and is fed by springs. The water was tested last year by the University of Saskatchewan and found to be in fit condition. Swimming parties are being organized which will be in charge of an Officer and will have several qualified swimmers holding life-saving certificates, to watch the swimming party.

Mowchenko Dam

Non-physical leisure time was also organized for personnel. From 1942 onwards, dances were a regular occurrence as the following logbook entry alludes to.

May 27, 1942: *A Station Dance and Entertainment Committee was formed for the purpose of organizing and carrying out a program of dances and entertainments. It is proposed, now that we have the Women's Division, to arrange a dance for each Saturday night for Airmen and Airwomen of the rank of Corporal and below, to be held in the Recreation Hall.*

Softball and baseball seem to have also been focal points of physical activity. A team of Mossbank airmen would periodically travel to Regina and Saskatoon to challenge other teams.

Sept 2, 1942: *The Station Men's Softball Team plays the RAF No. 33 EFTS Station at Caron, Sask., in the last of a play-off series. No.2 B&G School won.*

Sept 7, 1942: *The Station Baseball Team was in Regina today and played a double-header with the Regina Red Sox in the finals of the South Saskatchewan League. It being Labour Day, a large turn-out was on hand to see our team take the first game 4 to 3 and drop the evening game 1 to 0.*

Sept 11, 1942: *By winning two games from Saskatoon, No.2 B&G Men's Softball Team are Saskatchewan Intermediate Champions.*

C.O. Tennant at bat

In addition to physical activity, good food was also a priority. Arrangements were made for the Mossbank facility to grow vegetables for the mess hall on approximately 33 acres of land located across the road from the airbase. The land was owned by the Larson family. Crops included potatoes, peas, corn, tomatoes, cucumbers, beans, radishes, onions, beets, carrots, and lettuce. The following logbook entries make reference to this vegetable facility, which was called the "Victory Garden".

July 17, 1943: *The crop of radishes from the Victory Garden is almost exhausted but the green onions are next in order. The airmen and airwomen have enjoyed the fresh vegetables available every day.*

July 27,1943: *The Victory Garden shows very satisfactory growth but volunteer help is needed to keep ahead of the weeds. The members of the Women's Division were on duty at the garden tonight and other sections of the Station are ready to carry on during the next few weeks.*

August 31, 1943: *The last of the peas from the Victory Garden are being used and "Corn-on-the-Cob" is next on the list for camp consumption.*

July 4, 1944: *400 pounds of beets were taken from the Victory Garden today and delivered to the Airmen's Mess.*

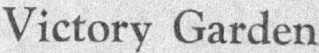

Victory Garden

How many at No. 2 B. & G. know that not far from the Control Tower can be seen another effort being made toward Victory. Yes, you have guessed it by this time, your Victory Garden and mine is going to produce, if we continue with the good work started, 33 acres of potatoes, peas, corn, tomatoes, cucumbers, beans, radishes, onions, beets, carrots and lettuce. In any effort toward VICTORY, it is the final results that count and whether the results obtained are good or bad depend on You and

You and You. A portion of the garden can be cared for by power machinery, but some of the smaller vegetables require hoeing and weeding.

If we are to derive the fullest benefit from Our Garden, it is essential that VOLUNTARY assistance be given.

A call goes out to everyone to volunteer to do one or two hours work during the next three months.

Just phone 22-1 or call at the Equipment Section and let them know when you are ready to begin.

CONTACT July 1943

In 1943, badminton, bowling, archery, movie and bingo nights were added to the roster of things to do when not on the job.

For readers who think that the concept of women's hockey is a recent development, it surely is not. The Mossbank facility had its own Women's Division hockey league.

Womens Hockey

Towards the end of 1943 and into 1944, recreation facilities continued to be developed. In January 1944, the bowling lanes were opened and a sheet of ice was created for outdoor curling. In the Summer of 1944, a swimming meet and a track and field meet were held. A cricket team was even put together.

August 20, 1944: The Station Cricket Team played the R.C.M.P. at Regina today. The game proved interesting with Regina receiving the highest number of runs.

August 31, 1944: F/O Schofield and the Aussies and the New Zealanders have shown great enthusiasm over cricket. They have traveled to Assiniboia, Moose Jaw, and Regina and were victorious against Regina on Sunday 27 August.

High Jump

Track Meet

CO Tennant Bowling

THE POWER OF THE WRITTEN WORD

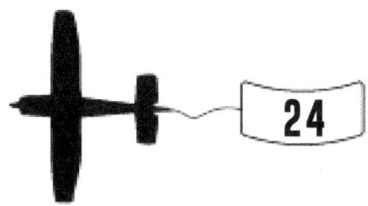

In the Spring of 1941, a group of airmen stationed at Mossbank No.2 realized that they had something in common. They had all previously worked for local newspapers in their hometowns. They proposed to the station Commander, A.J. Ashton, the idea of creating a paper to help make life a bit more cheerful.

On May 15, 1941, the first issue of *Contact – the Voice of the Dust Bowl Airport* came off the press at Model Printing in Gravelbourg. It was printed on paper 18 inches by 13 inches wide and distributed free of charge to all personnel. Local businesses in Mossbank were encouraged to purchase advertising space to help defray printing costs.

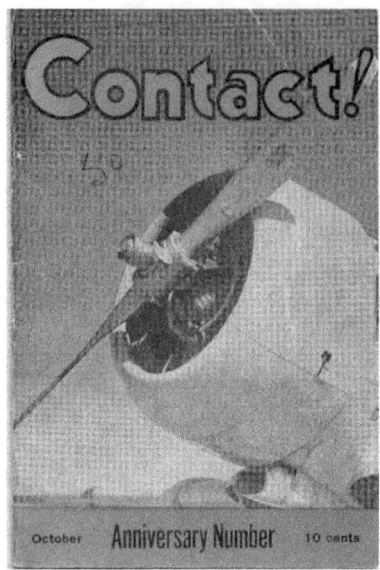

CONTACT! October 1941

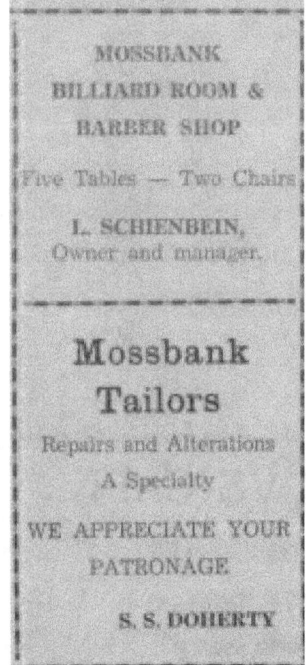

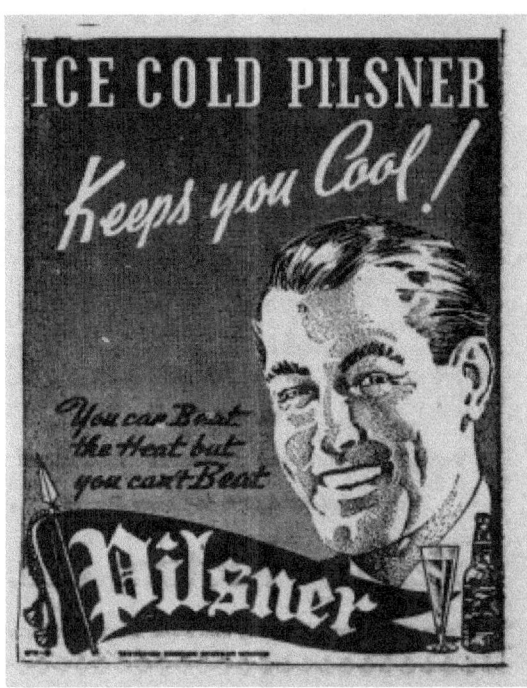

In the May 1941 issue, a Mossbank businessman wrote a piece for the paper expressing his gratitude for the airbase. The article read:

I take this opportunity in thanking the editor of the RCAF newspaper "Contact" for the privilege of saying a few words and to wish the editor and his associates every success in their new venture. The coming of the RCAF to our district was hailed with jubilation for this brought to us more than ever before the realization that the empire was at war.

No doubt the personnel were not enthusiastic at the prospect of being posted to No.2 Bombing and Gunnery School at Mossbank.

"Just where is this Mossbank?" they would ask, scanning maps and making exhaustive inquiries.

"It is a little-known town of some 300 souls", someone would reply, "about 50 miles south-west of Moose Jaw, where the people fought so valiantly for ten years against such adverse conditions as drought, pests, and poor crop conditions and stayed with it; where the "Golden Rule" was practiced every day, where the men banded themselves together, giving of their time and labour in beautifying the town, making it one of the best kept towns in Saskatchewan."

Be that as it may, everything was visibly brightened for Mossbank when the first transport carrying the boys "who ride the clouds" passed along Main Street and the first plane flew overhead, and it was a welcome and thrilling sight when the first boys in the now familiar "Airforce Blue" were seen on our streets.

From a purely business point of view, the RCAF has been our salvation. Work has been provided for a great number of our citizens, directly or indirectly. There has been a great increase in business and trade of every description. New Cafes have opened up and a new up-to-date Hotel – with the ten cent store as an added attraction – now holds a prominent place on Main Street.

The Movie Theatre has been enlarged with more and better accommodation, better pictures and other improvements to add to its attractions.

Although we realize that Mossbank cannot compete with the larger centres for things such as Parks, Rivers, Civic Centres, etc., we have attractive stores, good tennis courts, and a fine curling and skating rink, where dances are held in the summer months.

Then we have beautiful sunsets and beautiful girls too. There are warm and friendly hearts everywhere because we too are Canadians, and will not be found wanting in hospitality and service. And the people of the prairie are noted for their genuine big heartedness.

We have been very happy to welcome the wives and families of the members of the RCAF The housing problem was difficult at first, but gradually these things are all adjusting themselves and I would like to congratulate these ladies on their ability "to go forward under difficulties." They have proven to be good sports in taking all these things in their stride.

It has been a thrilling experience to the writer to shake hands with the boys from all over the empire and the United States. It has brought pleasant memories of the wonderful "Comraderie" that existed in the last war and is existing here today. We are proud to rub shoulders with the lads who are holding the torch on high today, and we want to do our utmost as citizens to make their stay among us a pleasant and happy one.

Yes, the old order in Mossbank is gone, but we are proud to say "Long may the new one live".

By 1942, *Contact* had grown in popularity. To make the paper easier to mail, the size was reduced to 8 x 12 inches. In May 1943, the decision was made to publish the paper on a regular monthly basis. Personnel could purchase the publication for 10 cents, affix a stamp to it and mail it to family members who were eager to know what life at Mossbank No.2 was like.

In the October 1943 issue of *CONTACT!* an article appeared that was titled *Third Anniversary:*

In October 1940, Mossbank welcomed the first contingent of airmen at the #2 B&G School. To most of us it was truly a great event. Who could have foreseen that the old dustbowl could have been transformed into what it is today – one of the finest RCAF stations in the Dominion of Canada.

And what has the school done for Mossbank? One cannot readily forget the conditions that existed through the long years of drought and depression, culminating in the resulting evils that followed in its wake — unemployment, and poverty. Like good westerners, Mossbank people took it on the chin, staying with the old ship; hoping for that "next year" that never seemed to come. But it did come with the first transport of boys to the #2 B&G School.

The Town changed almost overnight and became a hive of Industry. It certainly brought the war a little nearer to our doors. Transports and station wagons appeared in the streets and we saw the uniform of the RCAF everywhere. Merchants smiled again; new restaurants sprang up. Even the little 10 cent store around the corner came into its own.

There was a bustle and brightness everywhere. With the coming of the airmen's wives, the little Town boomed greater than ever. Rooming houses went up and houses and shacks that had been empty for years were brought in from the country and converted into clean and comfortable homes. Twelve new cottages were built by one enterprising citizen, several airmen brought their own "houses on wheels" with them, but in the meantime nearly all the good ladies of Mossbank shared their homes with the newcomers. Soon the first baby carriages appeared on the streets, and many of these children are now our youngest friends. Since then, countless babies have arrived from time to time.

Another exciting day in the life of Mossbank was the arrival of the first contingent of that fine body of women — the RCAF Women's Division- "who serve that men may fly." With their trim uniforms and smart appearance, they have added greatly to the attraction of the town. Together with the airmen's wives, our W.D.s have helped in no small way to restore good business to the town. The beauty parlours particularly have benefited. No 2 B&G School has also provided employment for many of our citizens, and this has added greatly to the happiness and welfare of our people.

BOMBS AWAY!

During the three years that we have had the RCAF with us, we have made many true and trusted friends whom it was a privilege to meet. Many of them are now overseas, several have already paid the supreme sacrifice, and there exists today a fine spirit of friendship and co-operation between the members of the RCAF and their wives and the good people of Mossbank.

In February 1944, a contest was organized to come up with a new name for the paper. The winning suggestion was *The Mossbank Target*.

The various issues of *CONTACT!* and *Target!* sometimes contained bits of news from Mossbank; some uplifting, some disheartening.

July 1943: *Masonic Lodge Worshipful Master William Mitchell reminds Brethren that the Lodge meets the first Wednesday before the Full Moon each month.*

April 1944 Issue

TARGET! Editorial Team

July 1943: *You are doing a wonderful service for the benefit of the youth of Mossbank by throwing open on Saturday afternoons the swimming pool for their use. Thank You.   The Mayor of Mossbank*

September 1943: *Owing to a shortage of teachers due to the war, Mossbank School has found itself handicapped. Nevertheless, the five students in Grade 12 all passed their final exams in June. The students are: Joyce Draper, Thelma Haight, Dorothy Stribbel, Iola Haug, and Winnifred Clarke. Successful Grade 11 exam candidates were Irene Sandbeck, Emma Nagel, Rose Tisdale, Joe McLaughlin, and Bob Olson.*

September 1943: *George Dunlop is the first to report having combined wheat. George is well pleased the way it is trickling through, yielding 25 bushels to the acre.*

October 1943: *Flight Officer Lawrence Dunlop, son of Mr. and Mrs. George Dunlop of Mossbank, was killed in action overseas on September*

7, 1942. He enlisted in the RCAF on September 25, 1941 and did his training at Calgary, Edmonton, High River, and Claresholme, Alberta. He received his wings March 4, 1942. He landed in England on December 24, 1942

November 1943: Mr. and Mrs. Henry Hutchinson have received news that their son , Robert James Hutchinson, had been wounded in action with the 8th Army. He had joined the 8th Army in July 1943.

April 1944: Mr. & Mrs. P.J. Rawlinson sold their hardware store to local resident Robert Balfour. The Rawlinsons are headed to the Pacific Coast to enjoy retirement. The Rawlinson's were prominent members of the community of Mossbank and were noted for their keen interest in the well-being of personnel stationed at Mossbank #2 B&G School.

July 1944: A wedding took place on Monday, July 3, 1944 at St. Andrew's Church in Moose Jaw. Audrey Jean Campbell, daughter of Mr. and Mrs. R.S. Campbell of Mossbank became the bride of Calvin Ross Sutor, eldest son of Mr. and Mrs. Calvin Sutor of Mossbank, Rev. Geoffry Glover officiated. The bride was lovely in a gown of white sheer over taffeta, Her veil was held in place by rose buds and she carried a bouquet of roses. She was attended by Ms. Irene Sandbeck. The groom was attended by his brother Steve Sutor. The wedding dinner was served in the Grant Hall Hotel. The table was centred with a three-tier wedding cake.

October 1944: The Mossbank tennis courts have been put in shape and new members are welcome. The fee for the season is $1.50 and is payable to the Secretary-Treasurer, Mr. F.B. Smith – C.N.R. Station Agent. C.N.R. Agent Smith is better known as a lover of tennis and a very enthusiastic curler. His family – two daughters and one son, have resided in Mossbank since 1940. Mr. Smith has always been public-spirited and has done his share on Mossbank's local committees.

Quite often the issues would contain brain teaser questions.

A man left $400 to be divided between his two sons, Harry and John. If one-third of John's inheritance is taken from one-fourth of Harry's, the remainder would be $44.

What is the amount of each son's inheritance?

During a bridge building effort, a pile was driven in the river. The foreman noted that at high water, 1/4 of the pile was embedded in the river mud, 1/3 was under water and the top of the pile was 17 feet, 6 inches above water. What is the length of the pole?

A maid is promised $100 plus a coat if she works for one year. She leaves her position after 7 months and is awarded $20 plus given the coat. How much is the coat valued at?

An aircraft flew at 180 miles per hour for 2 hours and then at 196 miles per hour for 3 hours. What was the average speed?

A pilot flew from 1033 hours to 1255 hours. What was his flying time in minutes?

Note: the answers to these brain teasers can be found in the Notes section for this chapter.

GERMANY FADES

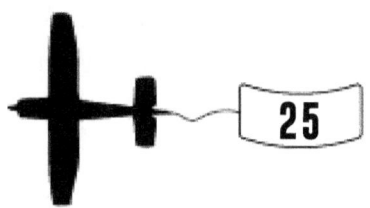

Operation Barbarossa took Soviet leader Stalin by surprise. The invasion involved nearly three million German troops, 3,000 tanks, 7,000 artillery pieces, and 2,500 aircraft. This was the largest invasion force in the history of warfare.

However, Hitler had not factored in the size of the Russian population. The Russians quickly shook off their surprise and countered the German invading force with an equal number of men. Taken aback by this development, Hitler wasted precious time arguing with his field commanders about strategy. His commanders wanted to press forward and take Moscow. Hitler wanted to take a side-excursion to capture the oilfields of the Caucassus region. Hitler recognized that oil was critical to the German war effort. It was getting its oil from Romanian fields and it was making synthetic fuel from lignite coal. Capturing the

Caucassus region would more than satisfy Germany's energy needs. Hitler split his troops. The contingent he sent to capture the Caucassus region ran out of fuel and supplies just as it reached its destination. A furious Hitler relieved his field commander of his duties.

By October, 1941, the contingent of German forces sent towards Moscow had managed to move within 200 miles of their target. But then the weather turned nasty. Temperatures plummeted and the Moscow area soon found itself in the grips of one of the earliest winters ever. The German troops were not prepared. They lacked warm clothing. The cold temperatures hindered the operation of tanks, aircraft, artillery and vehicles. Russian troops were well prepared for the elements. Over the course of the following month, Germany suffered about 730,000 casualties.

As the Barbarossa debacle was unfolding, Hitler's Luftwaffe was executing bombing raids on Exeter, Bath, Norwich, and York. At sea, German U-boats were sinking a reported 700,000 tons of British and American cargo each month in the Atlantic Ocean. On the surface Germany still looked menacing. But Hitler's military Generals knew the truth. British RAF bombers had destroyed much of the German cities of Lubeck, Cologne, Rostock, Bremen, Munich, Saarbrucken, and Hamburg. In addition, bombing attacks designed to destroy hydroelectric dams on the Ruhr river had been intensified. The release of the water behind the bombed dam structures flooded factories, coal mines, railways, roads, bridges, and towns downriver thus creating a setback for the German war effort. The flooding saw thousands of German civilians perish and tens of thousands left homeless. Naval vessels operated by Britain and the U.S. were equipped with radar which gave them a distinct advantage in locating the marauding U-boats in the Atlantic. By May 1943, the German Navy had withdrawn all its U-boats from the Atlantic. Germany was fading. It did not have the men or materials that would be needed to satisfy all of Hitler's grandiose goals.

However, Hitler was not ready to accept the reality that the German war machine was fading. He blindly ordered his commanders to keep up the fight and press deeper into Russia with whatever troops and equipment remained. His commanders did as they were told but the Russian Army was waiting for them. On January 8, 1943 a top Russian commander presented Hitler's commanders with an ultimatum. Get out of Russia or our guns will turn on you. Hitler flat out refused the ultimatum and told his field commanders that surrender was forbidden. On January 10, 1943 the Russians opened fire with 5,000 artillery guns. Three weeks later the German Army had been soundly defeated. This marked perhaps the greatest defeat a German army had ever endured.

But Adolf Hitler still would not quit. In response to the savage bombing assaults on the Ruhr valley hydroelectric dams, he launched the *Nazi New Order* which saw millions of Jewish people massacred at German concentration camps. If Hitler could not defeat Russia or Britain, then he at least wanted to cleanse Germany of undesirable elements, especially Jews.

In late November 1943, President Roosevelt, Prime Minister Churchill, and Soviet leader Stalin met in Tehran to discuss an all-out offensive in 1944 to once and for all defeat Germany. In the U.S., President Roosevelt decided to bring the Pacific conflict to an end when he authorized the Manhattan Project which would create the first ever atomic bomb.

Although not realized by the men and women serving at Mossbank No.2 Bombing and Gunnery School, Hitler was faltering. The war in Europe had just reached a tipping point.

At the end of 1942, Mossbank No. 2 had 71 Officers, 636 Airmen, 126 Airwomen, 268 Trainees, and 140 civilians. The troublesome Fairey Battles were now gone, replaced by 17 Lysanders, 22 Ansons, and 22 Bolingbrokes.

CAPTAIN BLAINE ASSUMES COMMAND

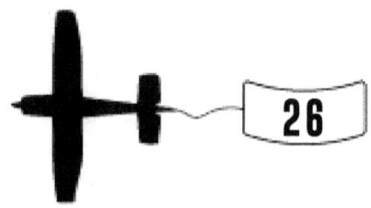

The start of 1943 brought new command to Mossbank. Group Captain D.S. Blaine would be in charge from January 1943 to October 1943.

Captain Blaine was born in New Brunswick but grew up in Bow Island, Alberta (west of Medicine Hat). He attended Royal Military College from 1928 to 1932, graduating with honours. He then went on to obtain a degree in Civil Engineering at Queen's University. After graduating from Queen's, he reported to Camp Borden for RCAF training. Prior to being assigned to Mossbank, he had been at No. 4 Training Headquarters in Calgary.

At Mossbank No.2, the primary focus continued to be that of quickly and efficiently graduating classes of student airmen. However, judging from comments in Captain Blaine's logbook, there seems to have been a secondary focus; a pivot towards embracing communities situated close to air training bases. In April 1943, the officers entertained 63 civilians from Mossbank and area to raise awareness of the training being done at the airbase.

Capt. D.S. Blaine

Also in April, two Carnival nights were held with civilians from the surrounding area invited. Blaine's logbook recorded the event:

April 17, 1943: The second Carnival night of the week took place in the Drill Hall; open to all and sundry. Hundreds of civilians from many miles around attended along with Service personnel to make a gala evening. Dancing, games of chance, hot dog stand operated by the Red Cross Society of Mossbank, all assisted in making fun and frolic for all. From this event, and the one held two days previous $1,900 was raised toward the many desired improvements being undertaken at this Unit.

The community outreach extended to Moose Jaw where the City declared Monday, May 24, 1943 to be the opening of Air Force Week.

Moose Jaw Air Force Week Parade

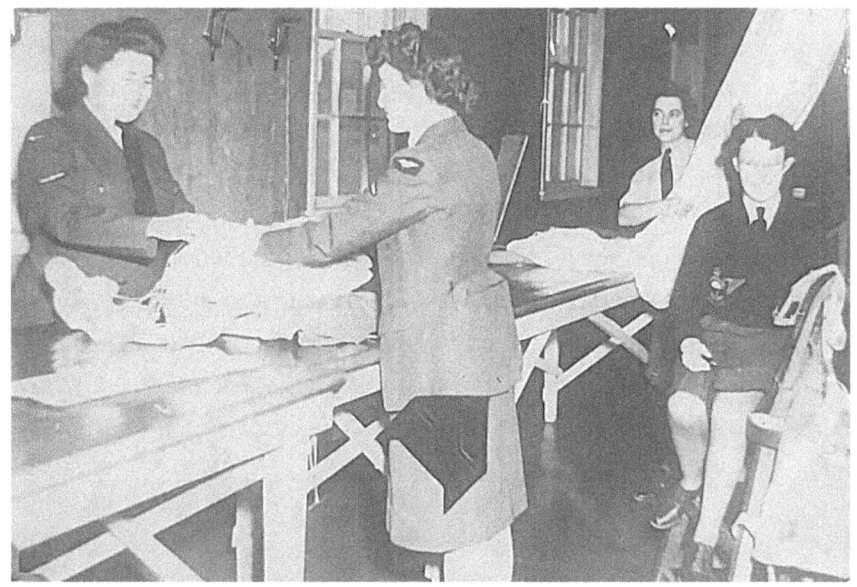

Parachute Packing

Blaine's logbook also describes a parachute packing demonstration given in Moose Jaw:

May 24, 1943: During this week, two Airwomen gave a demonstration of parachute packing in Joyner's Store daily at 14.30 hours. At the same time, an Airwoman was demonstrating the use of Wireless in Kresge's Limited.

The month of July saw another effort to engage citizens from the surrounding area.

July 14, 1943: This was a delightful day for the crowd of women from many points in Southern Saskatchewan who accepted the invitation to visit the camp for the "W.D. At Home". Some 500 ladies attended. The guests were welcomes by Group Captain D.S. Blaine and then they were conducted about the camp by W.D. guides who did an excellent job and answered many questions. Supper was served in the Airmen's Mess at

1600 hours and many comments were passed on the speed with which so many were served and also on the tastiness of the meal. No addition was made to the regular menu for this event and the guests were treated to a taste of camp life as they filed past the serving tables. The menu consisted of salad plate with cold meat and pickles, fruit cup with cake and tea. Visitors came from Moose Jaw, Regina, Assiniboia, Gravelbourg, Vantage, Ardill, Mossbank, Shamrock, La Fleche, Melaval, Lumsden, Crane Valley, Bishopric, and Markinch. The Press was represented by Miss Evans of the Moose Jaw Times and Miss Grassick of the Regina Leader Post. Miss Powell of C.J.R.W. Regina gathered material for a broadcast of the event. It was felt the afternoon was successful and that a definite amount of information regarding W.D. was sent over a large area.

CAPTAIN TENNANT ASSUMES COMMAND

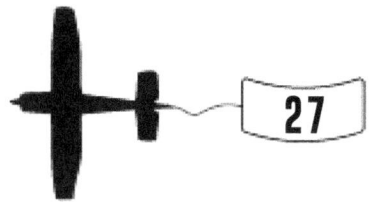

In early October 1943, Group Captain Blaine was assigned elsewhere. Wing Commander W.J. Bundy was brought in to temporarily to manage the Mossbank facility until the new Commander arrived. On October 6, 1943, Mossbank welcomed Group Captain E.C. Tennant. He would oversee the Station until its closing.

Tennant was born in Winnipeg, Manitoba. When he was two years old, his parents moved to Victoria, B.C. After graduating from high school, he took a job at the Imperial Bank in Golden, B.C. In 1915, he enlisted in the 47th Infantry Battalion of the Canadian Army. He was sent overseas where he served in France and Germany until June 1919. In February 1923, he joined the Canadian Air Force at Jericho Beach, Vancouver where he did his first flying as a Flight Engineer. He spent the next thirteen years flying fishery patrols on the west coast and forestry patrols in northern Manitoba. In 1937, he was posted to an RAF Armament School in Eastchurch, England. When war broke out, he returned to Canada where he conducted armament training for pilots being trained for overseas assignments. He was next assigned to Prince Rupert, B.C. as a Station Commander. His next posting was Mossbank where his focus would be on operational efficiency.

Group Captain E.C. Tennant

Under his command, Mossbank No.2 Bombing and Gunnery School twice won the Air Minister's Efficiency Pennant, was runner up once, and took honorable mention once.

Mossbank Efficiency Pennant

Flight Officer R.V. Webb, WD Commanding Officer 1942-1943

OPERATION OVERLORD

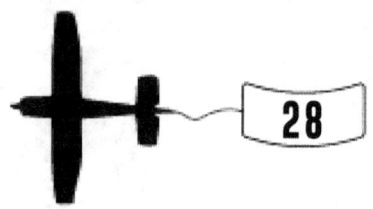

In 1943, the Allied countries began planning for an all-out assault on the heavily fortified beaches of Normandy in north-west France. The name of the attack would be Operation Overlord.

The Allies were confident that the operation would succeed and that Hitler would be vanquished. This sentiment is reflected in a log book entry from March, 1944 which announced that Mossbank would be closing by December 1944.

March 31, 1944: *The announcement of the Department of National Defence to the effect that this Station will be closed on December 1, 1944 is having a most demoralizing effect on many of our personnel. This is reflected by the increase in interviews respecting requests for "compassionate" postings and in many instances of requests for discharge to civilian life.*

On June 6, 1944 the Allied armies launched an aerial assault with 1,200 planes to rout the Germans. Fully 60 percent of the single-engine RAF aircraft were piloted by BCATP trained personnel. This assault was followed by an amphibious landing of over 150,000 troops and 23,000 paratroopers at five different beaches. This attack had been carefully orchestrated, even taking into account the brightness of the Moon and the tidal strength. The Germans were outnumbered. By the end of the month, The Allies were in charge with over 850,000 men and 148,000 vehicles in place. While these figures sound impressive, they came at a severe cost. Nearly 4,800 Allied troops lost their lives. The German army suffered losses of over 20,000 men.

> "THERE IS NO MOMENT NOW TO SLACK, HARD AS IT MAY SEEM, AFTER FIVE LONG YEARS OF WAR TO BRING THE SLAUGHTER TO AN END."
> – Winston Churchill on D-Day 1944

Despite the troop losses, Hitler still would not give up the fight. On December 16, 1944, he decided to launch a surprise attack in the Ardennes region of Belgium and Luxembourg (the *Battle of the Bulge*). At first the 400,000 German troops made good progress with cloudy skies helping to prevent Allied airplanes from spotting them. But several days later when the skies cleared, a U.S. armored division was ready to engage them. When the guns stopped blazing, over 60,000 Germans and nearly 9,000 Allied troops lay dead. Hitler was in serious trouble and this time he knew it.

By early 1945, advancing Russian troops had taken much of Poland and had moved to within 100 miles of Berlin. General Eisenhower's U.S. troops had closed in on Berlin as well. On April 28, 1945, Heinrich Himmler offered to surrender the Germany Army to the Americans. Adolf Hitler was stunned when he heard the news. He went silent when he was told that Russian troops were only several blocks away from his bunker in Berlin.

On April 29, 1945, Hitler summoned his personal secretary to write down notes. In typical narcissistic fashion, Hitler maintained that the great victories of the last several year had been due to him. Any battlefield failures were the fault of others.

End of War in Europe

Later that day, news arrived that Mussolini had been captured and executed in Italy. Disturbed by this news, Hitler flew into a rage; poisoned his favourite dog, and shot two other dogs. He instructed his personal secretary to destroy all papers in his personal files. He then shook hands with others who had assembled in the room, as if to say goodbye.

The next day, April 30, 1945, Hitler bid a final farewell to Goebbels and several of his military commanders. Hitler then retired to his bedroom along with his companion Eva Braun. Moments later a single shot was heard. Twelve years and three months after becoming Chancellor of Germany, Adolf Hitler was dead, aged 56 years old. Eva Braun lay motionless beside him; dead from having taken a cyanide poison pill. Their bodies were taken outside to the garden and lit on fire. The Third Reich was finished.

Adolph Hitler and Eva Braun

FAREWELL!

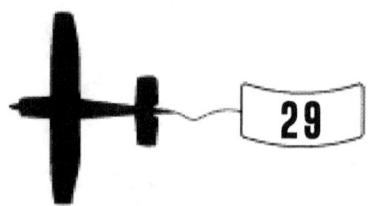

On October 14, 1944, the Department of National Defence formally issued *Organization Order No. 454* which ordered Mossbank No.2 Bombing and Gunnery School to become inactive as of December 1, 1944 and to disband effective December 15, 1944.

In response to the order, by October 31, 1944, Mossbank command had reduced the aircraft inventory to 17 Ansons, 10 Bolingbrokes, 7 Lysanders, and 1 Harvard. On November 3, the final group of airmen trainees were graduated and shipped out.

On November 22, 1944 all personnel remaining gathered for a farewell dinner. Group Captain Tennent's log entry describes the meal:

November 22, 1944: A full course Christmas dinner – turkey and all the trimmings, Christmas pudding with brandy sauce – yes, real genuine brandy, ice cream and Christmas cake.

Farewell Party

On December 6, all equipment, tools, and other articles that were not needed at other military facilities were auctioned off to the general public.

In December 1944, an article appeared in the *Lake Johnston Star* lamenting the closing of the Mossbank facility.

Well, the Airport closed! This brings to all of us a feeling of melancholy. A number of the air force personnel have been with us for a long time. It will be like pulling up roots to have them go. We believe this feeling will be shared, not only by the residents of Mossbank district but by the members of the air force as well. A great many lasting friendships have been built up and a goodly number of us feel that no matter where we go, we shall be able to look up friends whom we have met during the past four years. The presence of the airport has given us a broader outlook and has pulled a number of us out of the sort of provincialism that we had before the coming of so many fine people from every corner of the Earth. True, Mossbank has benefitted from the air force from a strictly business standpoint but more enduring, more up enduring, more uplifting, and more endearing have been the human contacts that have been made.

Mossbank No.2 Bombing and Gunnery School closed on the 15th of December 1944, having trained 2,539 bomber-aimers and 3,702 air gunners. In all, 21 men died, one female died, and one construction worker died.

The total cost of building Mossbank No.2 Bombing and Gunnery School was $1,116,402. Of this figure, the six hangar buildings accounted for nearly one-third of the project cost. In today's dollars the $1,116,402 figure would be close to $14 million, assuming such a project could be completed with the efficiency that Poole Construction exhibited in 1940.

On March 29, 1945, Prime Minister McKenzie King seized the political limelight and spoke glowingly about the BCATP. The following excerpts are from his speech:

"More than 150,000 men have graduated under the plan as trained aircrew. All of them have shared in that comradeship in arms which is perhaps the proudest possession among the great fraternity of fighting airmen. Not a few have laid down their lives in defence of the great cause of the world's freedom. They belong to the chivalry of God."

"When the principle of a joint air training plan was first agreed upon, the Right Hon. Neville Chamberlain, said "with the facilities, which Canada possesses, this cooperative effort may prove to be of the most essential and decisive character.""

"When the Right Hon. Winston Churchill spoke in this House of Commons chamber on December 30, 1941, he referred to "the wonderful and gigantic empire training scheme" as "another major contribution made by Canada."

"Throughout the perils and fortunes of war, fighting airmen trained in Canada have daringly and gallantly carried the battle for freedom with increasing vigour and effect far across and above enemy lines in all parts of the world. A sense of history surrounds the winding up of an enterprise as extensive and powerful as the British Commonwealth Air Training Plan has been. May the comradeship in arms be carried by our fighting airmen far beyond the days of war into the years of peace. Through the sovereign air may they continue to pass, not as messengers of winged death to those who have betrayed their fellow men, but as harbingers of peace for all mankind."

McKenzie King then read a message that he had received from British Prime Minister Churchill: "At this moment, when the memorable British Commonwealth Air Training Plan is being brought formally to an end, I send you, the Canadian government and the Royal Canadian Air Force, my warmest congratulations on the successful accomplishments of a spacious task imaginatively conceived and most faithfully carried out. This master plan has done much to speed us along the road to victory. In Canada alone, trained air crews, of whom more than half were Canadian, have been turned out at an average rate of twenty-five thousand a year over the last five years. Moreover, the quality of the training has been outstanding and has shown itself triumphantly in superiority which we have gained over the enemy in every type of air combat."

In September 1945, at the opening of a new session of the House of Commons, the Governor General, Lord Athlone, spoke: "It is just six years ago that Parliament met in special session in anticipation of a declaration of war. Since that time, war has been waged continuously, first against Germany, later also against Italy and Japan. From the very beginning, the resources of Canada and the utmost efforts of our people were committed to the fight for freedom and to the winning of victory. One by one, the aggressor nations and their satellite states have suffered total defeat by the armed forces of the United Nations. All have been compelled to surrender unconditionally."

In total, across Canada, the BCATP used 3,450 aircraft, employed 33,000 military personnel, and 6,000 civilians, and graduated over 131,000 trained aircrew. Of these graduates, 72,729 were members of the RCAF A total of 5,166 honors and decorations were awarded to RCAF personnel. Of these, 2,372 were Distinguished Flying Crosses and 433 were Distinguished Flying Medals.

Visitors to the Mossbank area who wish to drive through what was the Mossbank No.2 facility will see a plaque mounted to a cairn at the entrance to the site. The wording on the plaque reads:

THIS CAIRN IS DEDICATED IN MEMORY OF THOSE
WHO SERVED AT NO.2 BOMBING AND GUNNERY
SCHOOL, MOSSBANK DURING WORLD WAR II.

BETWEEN OCTOBER 28, 1940 AND DECEMBER 15, 1944,
THE SCHOOL TRAINED 2,539 AIR BOMBER AND 3,702 AIR
GUNNER STUDENTS OF WHOM 3,493 WERE CANADIAN, 1,651
AUSTRLIAN, 755 BRITISH, AND 342 NEW ZEALAND AIRMEN.

21 AIRMEN AND ONE AIRWOMAN DIED WHILE
SERVING AT THE SCHOOL AND ONE CONSTRUCTION
WORKER WAS KILLED DURING ITS MAKING.

THE SCHOOL'S PROUD MOTTO "AIM WELL – SHOOT
STRAIGHT" PERPETUATES THE DEDICTAION AND PURPOSE
OF THESE AIRMEN AND AIRWOMEN TO MAINTAIN DEMOCRACY
AND RESTORE PEACE THROUGHOUT THE WORLD.

"LEST WE FORGET"

Cairn Commemorating Mossbank No. 2

FINAL WORDS

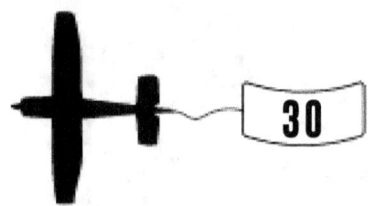

This book has taken the reader on a journey through an unsettled period of world history. The period of time from 1914 through 1944 was a harsh reminder that mankind is territorial and intolerant.

We want our turf and we will often resort to aggression to acquire territory owned by others.

Mankind also has a tendency to dislike those around it who have a different religious mindset or different cultural practices. Blinded by such intolerance, we can easily end up in conflict.

World War I was triggered by the breakdown of a precarious set of geopolitical alliances between the ruling empires of the day. After four years of fighting to near exhaustion, the hostilities stopped. Over 9 million soldiers had been killed. Millions more military personnel had been injured. Millions of civilians had also been killed or injured.

An attitude of intolerance then resurfaced when delegates to the Paris Peace Conference crafted the *Treaty of Versailles* which attempted to pin the blame and also the cost of the war on Germany. As the German economy faltered under the weight of the strict repayment schedule, a far-right activist by the name of Adolf Hitler promised to make Germany great again. His oratory skill attracted large crowds to his political rallies. German citizens who were feeling abandoned by the failing economy voted for his Nazi Party.

Once elected to power on the promise of making Germany great again, his hunger for European and indeed world domination was placed on display alongside his hatred and intolerance for other nations and for people of different religious and cultural beliefs.

European aristocracy along with elected officials from various nations decided the best approach in dealing with him would be one of appeasement. This strategy proved a spectacular failure. While global leaders dithered, Adolf Hitler took control of Austria and Czechoslovakia. He then turned the might of the German military against Poland. In short order, continental Europe had been trodden upon by Hitler's Nazi movement. Britain soon found itself staring head-on at the possibility of defeat by Hitler's forces.

A plea for help echoed through the British Commonwealth. Canada, Australia, and New Zealand responded by entering into the British Commonwealth Air Training Plan (BCATP). This plan saw flight schools as well as bombing and gunnery schools hastily built across Canada to train pilots, navigators, gunners, and bomb aimers. It was the BCATP that ultimately saved Britain and indeed the Commonwealth.

BOMBS AWAY!

The small farming community of Mossbank, Saskatchewan played a key role in the BCATP. The Mossbank No.2 Bombing and Gunnery School built at a cost of over $1 million in 1940, trained 2,339 Air Bombers, and 3,702 Air Gunners for the war effort. The School operated from 1940 until 1944. The success of the BCATP effort demonstrated that Canadians have a unique ability to meet a challenge head-on in a time of crisis.

This book was written to underscore how Canadians in 1940 rose to meet head-on the challenge of a fascist dictator. This book was designed to take readers on a journey through the four years of the Mossbank No.2 Bombing and Gunnery School. This historical journey is made meaningful through comments extracted from the Mossbank No.2 Commander's logbook and by photographs sourced at Archives Saskatchewan.

Unfortunately, time has a habit of letting the events of history and the lessons learned escape. Even though communities build museums to commemorate history, as time marches on people stop visiting them. People stop looking back at past events thinking that history will never repeat. The geopolitical events being experienced around the world at the present time, especially those events driven by policy emanating from Washington, should serve as a reminder that history can and will repeat.

This book was also written to provide commentary on the politics surrounding World War I, the *Treaty of Versailles*, the events that paved the way for the rise of the far-right in Germany, the failure to appease this far-right movement, and the subsequent outbreak of the World War II conflict. Hopefully this commentary will be embraced by educators who are responsible for shaping the minds and attitudes of the next generation of citizens.

Awareness of past historical events can help to chart a more desirable course for the future. Let us hope that we never have to witness a repeat of the events of the first decades of the 20th century. But if we do, Canadians will no doubt meet the challenge head-on with elbows up.

APPENDIX 1

THE PLANES OF MOSSBANK NO.2 BOMBING AND GUNNERY SCHOOL

FAIREY BATTLE

Fairey Battle Trainer No. 1703 - Mossbank

- Length: 42 ft 4 in
- Wingspan: 54 ft
- Power: 1030 hp each
- Engine: 1 x Rolls-Royce Merlin III
- Maximum Speed: 252 mph
- Cruising Speed: 200 mph
- Service Ceiling: 25,000 ft
- Range: 1,000 miles

In late 1940 an inventory of Fairey Battle Trainers began arriving at Mossbank. During 1941 records show that at any time there were between 50 and 60 Fairey Battle aircraft at Mossbank.

The Fairey Battle was a single-engine craft designed and built between 1936 and 1940 by British company Fairey Aviation for use as a bomber. The question of why these planes were sent to Canada was answered for this author during a telephone interview with 92-year-old Herb Arndt, who grew up on a farm not far from Mossbank No. 2. As a young lad full of curiosity, one day he ventured over to get a closer look at these planes. He noted that they all had what appeared to be patches on them. He later learned that at the outbreak of hostilities the Fairey Battles sustained substantial bullet damage from Hitler's Luftwaffe. Unsuitable for combat duty, the planes were pulled from RAF service and sent to Canada as training aircraft. A total of 739 Fairey Battles were sent to Canada, retrofitted with turrets, and used as bombing and gunnery trainers under the BCATP.

Some of the log book entries by Commander Ashton and his successors reflect the sentiment that the Fairey Battle Trainer was unsuitable, even as a training aircraft.

December 8, 1940: Fairey Battle No. L 5032, departed from Winnipeg, Manitoba, enroute to No.2 Bombing and Gunnery School, Mossbank, Saskatchewan, piloted by F/O B.P.M. Keenan. Near Virden, Manitoba, owing to engine failure and not being able to attempt a forced landing due to vision being obscured by fumes and smoke in cockpit, pilot bailed out at low altitude, hitting the ground with some force. Injuries to pilot consisted of multiple contusions, teeth loosened, and marked nervous strain.

February 8, 1941: Fairey Battle 1704 piloted by Flying Officer J.R. Bryan made a forced landing on the Bombing Range due to an air lock in the gas line.

March 14, 1941: Fairy Battle 1768 forced landing on Lake Johnston. Aircraft ran out of petrol, damage slight, personnel uninjured.

April 11, 1942: Flight Sergeant Edward B. Sexsmith was seriously injured and LAC G. Barnholden and LAC J.A. Kilpatrick were slightly injured when Fairey Battle 1900 piloted by Sexsmith caught fire and force landed on the Bombing Range. The aircraft was gutted by fire.

May 11, 1941: *Battle 1777 piloted by Flying Officer Lindsay blew a tire when landing, causing the aircraft to go up on its nose and damaging the airscrew.*

Fairey Battle No. 1777 Nose Down

May 21, 1941: *Battle No. 1690 piloted by Flying Officer L.M. James force landed 15 miles northwest of the aerodrome. The cause was engine failure.*

June 2, 1941: *Battle No. 1732 piloted by Flying Officer A.M. Vandre and with LAC Myles, W.R. and LAC McAlary N.B., as passengers, landed about 10 miles northwest of the aerodrome. Cause, broken glycol connection.*

June 7, 1941: *Battle No. 1652, piloted by Flying Officer G.H. Wolf, blew a tire in taking off and damaged the airscrew.*

LAC Donen and LAC Grier (the two trainees who parachuted to safety)
Airwoman Cpl. Barrette (who had packed their parachutes)

June 20, 1941: Fairey Battle No. 1756 made a forced landing near No.2 Target at Lake Johnston. The aircraft was not damaged, the forced landing was caused by a leak in the coolant tube.

October 18, 1941: Sergeant Pilot J.W. Hermiston made a very good job of force landing Battle aircraft #1766 this morning when his engine stalled.

May 6, 1942: At 2345 hours, during night flying exercises, a Battle aircraft developed a glycol leak and the pilot ordered the two trainees to bail out. The pilot landed the aircraft at the aerodrome. The jump was made at 5,000 feet, very dark, no Moon, no wind. A search party of 100 was organized. One of the boys walked onto road an hour later carrying his chute. The second was met by the search party little later.

Crane Being Taken to Crash Site

May 18,1942: An accident to Battle aircraft No.1649 occurred over Lake Johnston. The pilot stated he was practicing forced landings, raised his flaps and the subsequent drop of the aircraft brought it down to water level where one wing dipped in and the tip damaged by striking the lake bottom (only a few inches of water in the lake).

March 9, 1943: While carrying out a routine gunnery exercise, pilot F/Sgt Beatty, G.F. had his engine fail due to internal glycol leak and bearing failure and force landed with wheels retracted. No one was injured. The accident occurred three miles N.E. of Ardill using a Fairey Battle Mk I. The engine and propeller were severely damaged.

When a plane landed with its wheels retracted, the Station would dispatch a crane to the landing site using a trailer.

Lifting a Downed Fairey Battle

The weather posed on ongoing challenge for airmen training schedules. The following logbook entries express a certain amount of tongue-in-cheek sarcasm towards the weather.

June 12, 1941: The past 12 days have been wet, cold, and cloudy. The sun, during this time has hardly been seen. It is hard to convince those who are strange to these parts that we are situated in the heart of the prairie "Dust Bowl." The expression "Most unusual weather" is getting to be a joke around the Station and our newcomers are beginning to think they are having their legs pulled.

November 14, 1941: A dust storm raged north east south and west all day. Now the newcomers know why this is called the Dust Bowl.

As an aside, a logbook entry of June 1942 notes that southern Saskatchewan had been in a severe drought for many years.

June 17, 1942: Today has seen a continual series of heavy rain showers with a N.W. wind from 50 to as high as 70 m.p.h. and very cold. It will be interesting to see the precipitation figures for these two days. After 12 or 13 years of almost drouth conditions in this part of the Province, this Spring has been a complete reversal as far as moisture goes…

NORSEMAN

Norseman No.2463 – Mossbank

- Length: 32 ft 4 in
- Wingspan: 51 ft 6 in
- Power: 600 hp
- Engine: 1 x Pratt & Whitney R-1340-AN1
- Maximum Speed: 165 mph with wheels
- Cruising Speed: 141 mph with wheels
- Service Ceiling: 17,000 ft
- Range: 932 miles

The Noorduyn Norseman was designed by Robert Noorduyn in Montreal in the mid-1930s as a rugged transport plane. Until 1940, Noorduyn had sold only 17 Norseman aircraft, mainly to commercial operators in Northern Canada and to the RCMP. However, once the war started, the RCAF ordered 38 Norsemen as Wireless and Navigational trainers for the BCATP.

During 1941, records show that, at any time, up to two Norseman aircraft were at Mossbank Station. These Norseman were used for transport and general duties. In addition, they were used to orient new gunners and bomb aimer trainees to the targets on Lake Johnston.

AVRO ANSON

- Length: 42 ft 3 in
- Wingspan: 56 ft 6 in
- Power: 450 hp each
- Engine: 2 x Pratt & Whitney R-985-14B Wasp Junior
- Maximum Speed: 190 mph
- Cruising Speed: 174 mph
- Service Ceiling: 20,500 ft
- Range: 1,600 miles

Avro Anson No. 8240 Being Pulled from the Hangar

Avro Anson in Flight at Mossbank No.2

The Avro Anson ("Anson") was used by the BCATP to train pilots on dual-engine aircraft and to train bomb aimers. The first Ansons (Mark I) were shipped disassembled from England and reassembled in Canada using Canadian-built parts. After 1940, however, the British were no longer able to supply airframes and engines in the quantity required. To ensure availability, Anson production was set up in Canada. Between 1941 and 1944, over 1,800 Anson Mark II planes were built in Canada by a number of manufacturers.

Avro Anson cockpit

Aug 24, 1943: At 1640 hrs an accident occurred 14 miles west and 6 miles north of Gravelbourg, Sask., when Anson No. 7431 hit the top of a house and crashed. The pilot, Sgt. George Bertram Warren and Air Bomber LAC Thomas Millard were killed. The accident occurred during a routine bombing exercise and resulted from low flying.

HARVARD

- Length: 28 ft 11 in
- Wingspan: 42 ft
- Power: 600 hp
- Engine: 1 x Pratt & Whitney Wasp R-1340-AN-1
- Maximum Speed: 180 mph
- Cruising Speed: 140 mph

Harvard aircraft were used to help pilots transition from low-powered craft like the Tiger Moth to high-performance craft like the Spitfire. Noorduyn Aviation of Montreal produced nearly 2800 Harvard Mark II craft between 1940 and 1945. Records show that Mossbank usually had one Harvard aircraft in its inventory.

Harvard (restored version)

Harvard on the Tarmac

January 19, 1942: *Today at approximately 1430 hours, our Harvard No. 3797 crashed near Briercrest, Sask. Flight Lieutenant J.A. Peterson and Flying Officer C.F. Lawson were killed. This contributes the first fatal crash since the Station was opened nearly fifteen months ago. A total of over 32,000 hours has been flown—averaging 16,000 hours to a fatality. Flight Lieutenant J.A. Peterson was a Senior Administration Officer. He was a veteran of the last war and wore wings – having served with the RAF He was one of the most popular Officers and enjoyed the confidence of all.*

BOLINGBROKE

Bolingbroke No. 9912 – Mossbank

- Length: 42 ft 9 in
- Wingspan: 56 ft 4 in
- Power: 920 hp
- Engine: 2 x Bristol Mercury XV
- Maximum Speed: 288 mph
- Cruising Speed: 200 mph
- Service Ceiling: 27,000 ft
- Range: 1,400 miles

In September 1939, the first Bolingbroke Mark I aircraft was produced by Fairchild Aircraft of Longueuil, Quebec. It was a close copy of the Bristol Blenheim aircraft produced in Britain. The Bolingbroke Mark IV design was used by the RCAF for reconnaissance bomber training. As of July 1942, there were 12 Bolingbroke aircraft at Mossbank. As the following logbook entries indicate, the Bolingbroke was not without its problems.

Bollingbroke Cockpit

November 10, 1942: *An accident occurred at 1745 hours on aerodrome. Pilot P/O S.R. Vivian. Aircraft No. 9917 Bolingbroke. After taking off the pilot tried to get the wheels in the "up" position and found that the wheels had only retracted about three-quarters of the way. He then selected the wheels "down" position and found that the undercarriage would not lock. Various ways were then tried to raise and lock the undercarriage with no success. Belly landing resulted. Airscrews damaged and airscrew shaft out of alignment on both engines. Fuselage buckled. Underside of fuselage badly damaged. Both undercarriage jacks broken.*

December 14, 1942: *A fatal accident occurred at 1115 hours, five miles west of Lumsden, Saskatchewan, when six airmen of this Unit were killed instantly when aircraft No. 9984 Bolingbroke crashed into side of hill. The deceased: Pilot WO2 Everard Barrington North; Electrician LAC Robert Edwin Habkirk; AC1 Henry Vernon Pratt; LAC Howard Austin Lightle; LAC Russel Herman Schults; and LAC John Campbell. They were carrying out a routine airframe and engine test flight. The aircraft was a total loss with the exception of the tires and wheels and some electrical switches.*

February 2, 1943: An accident occurred one mile north-west of the Control Tower at 1735 hours with no injuries to personnel. The pilot was F/S H.S. Beckett, passengers being LAC J.S. Nulock, J.S., LAC I.A. Morris-Jones, LAC S.C. Berkely. Aircraft – Bolingbroke No. 9892. While carrying out a routine Gunnery Exercise, aircraft force landed due to engine failure. Starboard propeller shaft back to reduction gear broke off in air.

February 28, 1943: An accident occurred nine miles northwest of Mossbank at 1100m hours. No one injured. While carrying out a routine splash target gunnery exercise, the port engine failed at 200 feet. The pilot attempted to fly on starboard engine but used only normal five pound boost. Aircraft then gradually lost height and pilot force landed with undercarriage retracted. The damage consisted of the nose of the fuselage being pushed out of alignment. Lower portion of fuselage belly scraped and torn.

April 20, 1943: An accident occurred at 1020 hours here on the main aerodrome when F/O R.C. Charlton, pilot of the aircraft, noticing that the wheels failed to lock down, force landed on aerodrome with wheels retracted. The aircraft was Bolingbroke No.10120. No one was injured. The damage to aircraft consisted of propellers being curled on tips, undercarriage bent and under portion of aircraft scraped.

April 24, 1944: At 0900 hours Bolingbroke No. 9914, Pilot F/O Foster, force landed. When cruising at about 6000 ft. port engine started to miss and vibrate badly, finally cutting out entirely. Pilot fired two red flares over field-emergency. Aircraft landed on single engine.

November 24, 1943: An accident occurred at 1725 hours on Main Aerodrome. Aircraft Bolingbroke No. 9916. Pilot was Sgt. W.J. Kasubeck. Bombardiers were LAC P.J. Barake, LAC J.T. Griffiths. When attempting to land on return exercise, pilot was caught in sudden snow squall. Aircraft *and pitot head iced. Landed on runway and overshot same. Ran into rough ground, undercarriage collapsed, bad weather responsible for pilot overshooting runway on landing. Undercarriage buckled. Portion of wings and spar also buckled. Two propellers bent at tips. Engine damage not definitely ascertained at this time.*

March 13, 1944: *Bolingbroke No. 10111 crashed two miles south of field. Fatal – all crew members casualties. Killed were Pilot Officer V.H. Inderbitzen (age 24, Tacoma, WA), Sergeant H.M. Reed (age 21, Alameda, Sask), Leading Aircraftman J.E. Tierney (age 23, Vancouver, BC), Leading Aircraftman D.C. McKenzie (Age 21, Nailsworth, South Australia) and Leading Aircraftman K.R. McPherson (Age 20, Northcote, Victoria, Australia).*

All that the accident investigation revealed was that Bolingbroke No. 10111 was returning from a gunnery exercise and was flying at 800 feet when it suddenly dove straight into the ground two miles south of the Mossbank facility. The following images illustrate the severity of the crash.

Herb Arndt, an elderly gentleman from Medicine Hat. Alberta, remembers this incident like it happened yesterday. The crash site was near the farm he grew up on. He recalls that he and a couple of his school buddies rode their bicycles to the crash site. He recalls that his school buddies had nightmares for quite some time afterwards. Mr. Arndt claims to have found the broken pieces of a wristwatch in the wreckage. He says the hands on the watch indicated several minutes past 10:00 a.m., the time of the crash.

Bolingbroke No. 10111 Crash Site

Bolingbroke No. 10111 Crash Site

March 17, 1944: *Funeral services for LAC McPherson, and LAC McKenzie, escort and firing squad made up of Australians from Courses 75 and 76 W.A.G.*

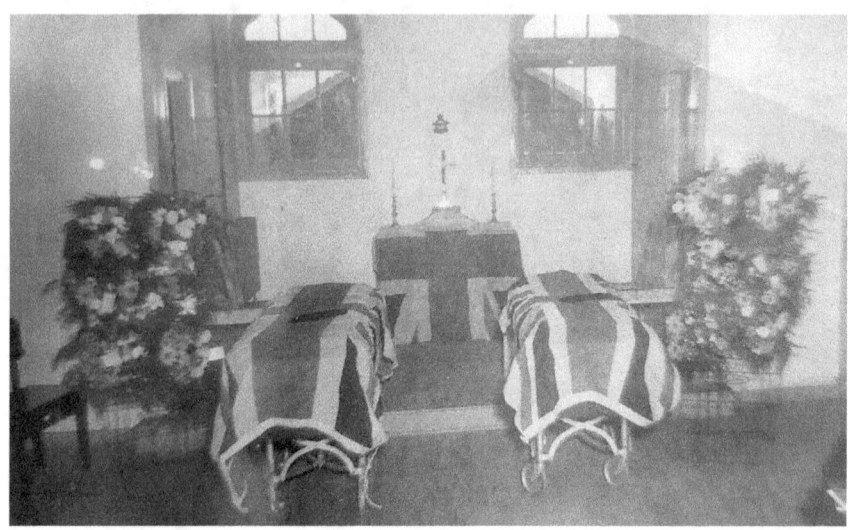

Caskets of LAC McPherson and LAC McKenzie in the Chapel

Funeral Procession for LAC McPherson and LAC McKenzie
(heading north along Main Street towards the cemetery)

Burial ceremony for LAC McPherson, and LAC McKenzie

Mrs. McPherson (accompanied by her daughter) made the trip
from Australia to visit her son's gravesite

In September 2001, Arni Olafson delivered a presentation at a meeting of the Regina, Saskatchewan chapter of the Canadian Aviation History Society. He shared with the audience several of his memories of his brief time at the Mossbank facility.

He arrived in Mossbank in February 1944 as a staff pilot, flying the station's Anson and Bolingbroke aircraft. He recalls that Avro Anson aircraft were used for the training of bomb-aimers and Bolingbroke aircraft were used for gunnery training. He described how a Bolingbroke or Lysander would put a drogue 300 feet behind it while other Bolingbrokes flew parallel to the drogue while student airmen opened fire from their turrets at the drogue. Each Bolingbroke carried three trainee gunners, each with their own colored rounds of ammunition. Matching the holes in the drogue with the colors used indicated each trainee's score.

For bombing and air-to-ground firing, the station used targets moored in Old Wives Lake, north of Mossbank. Forty minutes were allocated for each flight. Practice bombs gave a puff of smoke by day and a flash by night.

He recalled at least three fatal accidents at the station, one of them killing a pilot, an instructor and three students, two of whom were Australian. After the war, the mother of one the killed Australian's made the long journey to view his grave in Mossbank.

Weather was a factor even for the Bolingbroke aircraft. Arni recalled a night-time bombing instruction flight that took place under the imminent threat of bad weather. After dropping their bombs, they headed for base, where the gathering winds had already blown out all but one landing flare. As he came in to land, a gust of wing caught his right wing, sending it upward and lowering the port wing. He opened up the engines, straightened out, then landed the plane. The students aboard were shaken up and patted him on the back with gratitude.

Arnie Olafson

LYSANDER

Lysander 2343 Mossbank

- Length: 30 ft 6 in
- Wingspan: 50ft
- Power: 870 hp
- Engine: 1 x Bristol Mercury XX
- Maximum Speed: 212 mph
- Cruising Speed: 55 mph
- Service Ceiling: 23,800 ft
- Range: 1300 miles

In 1935, British company Westland Aircraft designed the Lysander for short take-off and landing (STOL) applications. The British RAF used Lysanders for night missions to fly undercover agents into occupied France and Belgium and to retrieve escaped prisoners of war (POWs).

By 1941, National Steel Car in Hamilton, Ontario was producing Lysanders for both the RAF and RCAF. The British Commonwealth Air Training Plan (BCATP), purchased 225 Lysanders for towing drogues at gunnery training schools.

A drogue resembled a large cylindrical kite, approximately 30 feet long and about 3 feet diameter. Construction material was a lightweight fabric made from cotton and silk. Once airborne, the drogue operator would release a 300 foot cable with the drogue attached to the end of the cable.

Airmen trainees in a Bolingbroke aircraft flying parallel to the Lysander would shoot bullets at the drogue target. The bullets were loaded with a color dye with each airman having different coloured bullets. Back on the ground, a team of airwomen would tally the number of colored impact sites.

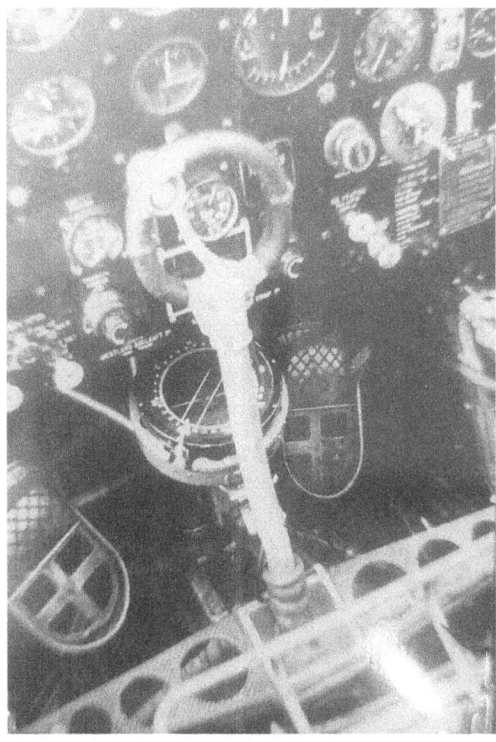

Lysander Cockpit

By July 1942, there was 10 Lysander aircraft at Mossbank. The following logbook entries show that there were incidents and accidents with Lysander aircraft as well.

November 9, 1942: *An accident occurred fifteen miles south of Mossbank aerodrome on Lake of the Rivers at 1620 hours. Aircraft Westland Lysander No.2342. Pilot was Sergeant E.H. Reilly. Drogue Operator was LAC V.A. Brody. Pilot refused permission to land for about eight minutes pending laying of flare path. Flew some miles till fuel ran out. Force landing in the ice-covered swamp. No injuries. Port and starboard wings are sprung and two propeller blades bent. Wheel farings torn considerably. The fixed fin is torn away from the fuselage. The engine at this date appears to be unserviceable.*

May 27, 1943: *At 1005 hours Lysander No. 1567, F/O J.R. Calderwood, crashed one-half mile east of Bishopric. Pilot suffered broken leg and head injuries. While awaiting gunnery aircraft, motor quit, pilot attempted forced landing, wheels hit a small knoll and plane turned over. Aircraft was a total loss.*

Lysander No.1567 turned over

January 24, 1944: *Lysander No.2369 and Bolingbroke No. 10075 collided two miles north-west of No. 1 Target, Johnston Lake. Both occupants of the Lysander Pilot P/O William Russel Stephens and Drogue Operator LAC Arthur Madiuk were killed. The two students from the Bolingbroke parachuted to safety.*

Lysander No.2369 / Bolingbroke 10075 Wreckage Site

APPENDIX 2

MATHEMATICS FOR AIRMEN

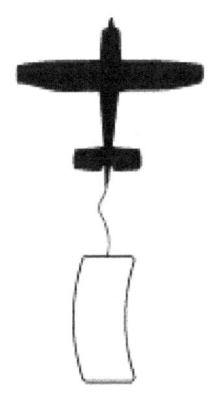

FLYING ON COURSE

The pilots flying the bomber-training aircraft had already taken their flight training elsewhere prior to being posted to Mossbank No.2. One of the particular skills necessary to fly bombing raids is the ability to adjust the plane's heading, groundspeed, and airspeed to compensate for wind direction so as to take an aircraft over its intended targets. For this, pilots had to be skilled in basic physics and trigonometry. The following mathematical example illustrates the rigors of trigonometry calculations.

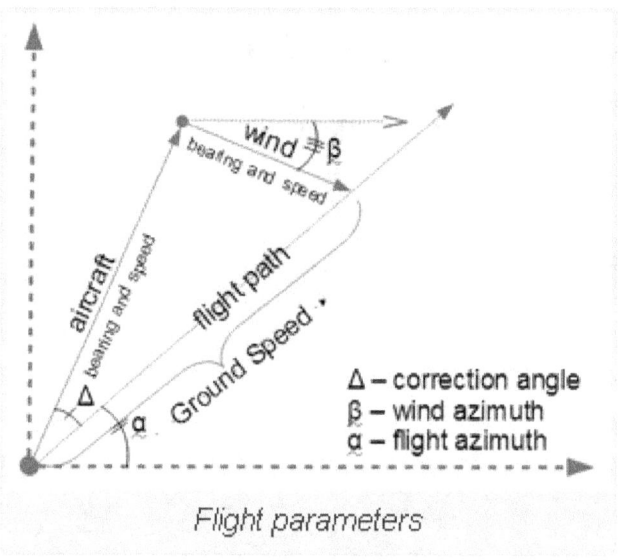

Flight Trigonometry

Suppose a plane is flying at 80 meters/second on a heading of N 30 degrees East. The wind is blowing from from a bearing of degrees at 10 meters/second.

Using the Law of Cosines, v^2 (ground) = v^2 (air) + v^2 (wind) − 2[v(air) * v(wind)cos(wind)], the equation yields: v^2 (ground) = (80)2

+ (10)2 – 2[(80)(10)cos(300)]. Therefore, the ground speed is 78.1 meters/second.

The *Law of Sines* can then be used to calculate how much the plane is drifting off course due to the wind. Sin (drift angle)/10 = sin 300/78.1. This equation yields a drift angle of 6.3. Therefore, the pilot is actually flying N 36.3 degrees East. If he wants to fly over the intended target so his bombardier can drop bombs, he needs to alter his course by 6.3 degrees.

BOMBING – IN THEORY

Airmen training to be bomb aimers (bombardiers) also had to be skilled in the mathematics of physics and trigonometry. A bomb released from a moving aircraft will follow a parabolic trajectory as it hurtles towards the ground. There is a horizontal and a vertical component to the parabolic trajectory of a falling bomb.

Suppose a bombing aircraft is flying towards Lake Johnston at 80 meters per second (179 mph). The plane is 1,500 meters above the ground (5000 feet). The horizontal component of motion is given by: $d=0.5 \, g \, t^2$; where g is the gravitational constant of 9.81 m/sec^2.

Putting numbers in this equation gives: $1,500 = 0.5 \, (9.81) \, t^2$. Solving the equation for t shows that the bomb will hit the target 17.48 seconds after release.

To determine the horizontal distance the bomb will follow during its parabolic trajectory, the equation d=V*t is used; where V is the speed of the plane. Putting numbers in this equation yields d=80 x 17.48. Solving for the variable d gives 1,398.4 meters (1,488 feet).

BOMBING – IN REALITY

Idealized examples on paper are one thing. Dropping a bomb from a moving aircraft over a target is quite another. Trying to hit a target below was complicated by aircraft speed, wind direction, wind speed, temperature, air density, turbulence, bomb launch angle, and distance to the target.

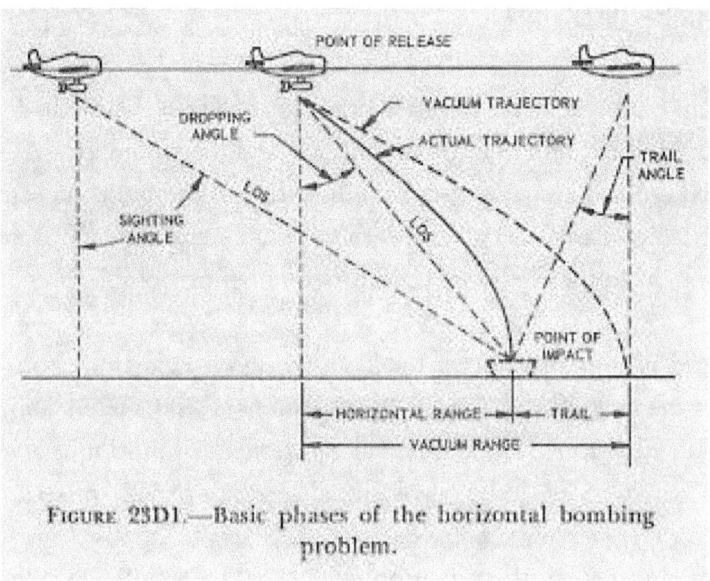

FIGURE 23D1.—Basic phases of the horizontal bombing problem.

Bomb Aiming

A bomb aimer was taught to use a bomb sighting device. There were many different designs of these devices used in World War II, all equipped with stabilizing gyroscopes. As the aircraft was heading towards its target, the bomb aimer would use the sighting device to measure the angle between the line of sight to the target and the true vertical. This was called the "sighting angle".

Student Airmen in Classroom

By adjusting the sighting device to account for bomb weight, bomb dimensions, airspeed, and windspeed, the aimer could quickly determine the dropping angle at which he should release the bomb. At the instant in time when the sighting angle and dropping angle were the same, the aimer would release the bomb.

Loading the bombs onto aircraft was not a task to be taken lightly. The following logbook entries make this very clear.

April 28, 1944: A bomb, accidently released from aircraft on the ground, injured A.C.1 Garden, who was on duty at the time. The accident happened at 1047 hours and ambulance called immediately. Ambulance arrived in under 2 minutes.

April 30 1944: One airman injured in bomb explosion, requiring amputation of left hand. Three patients required treatment for exposure and minor lacerations.

THE TRIGONOMETRY OF BOMBING A TARGET

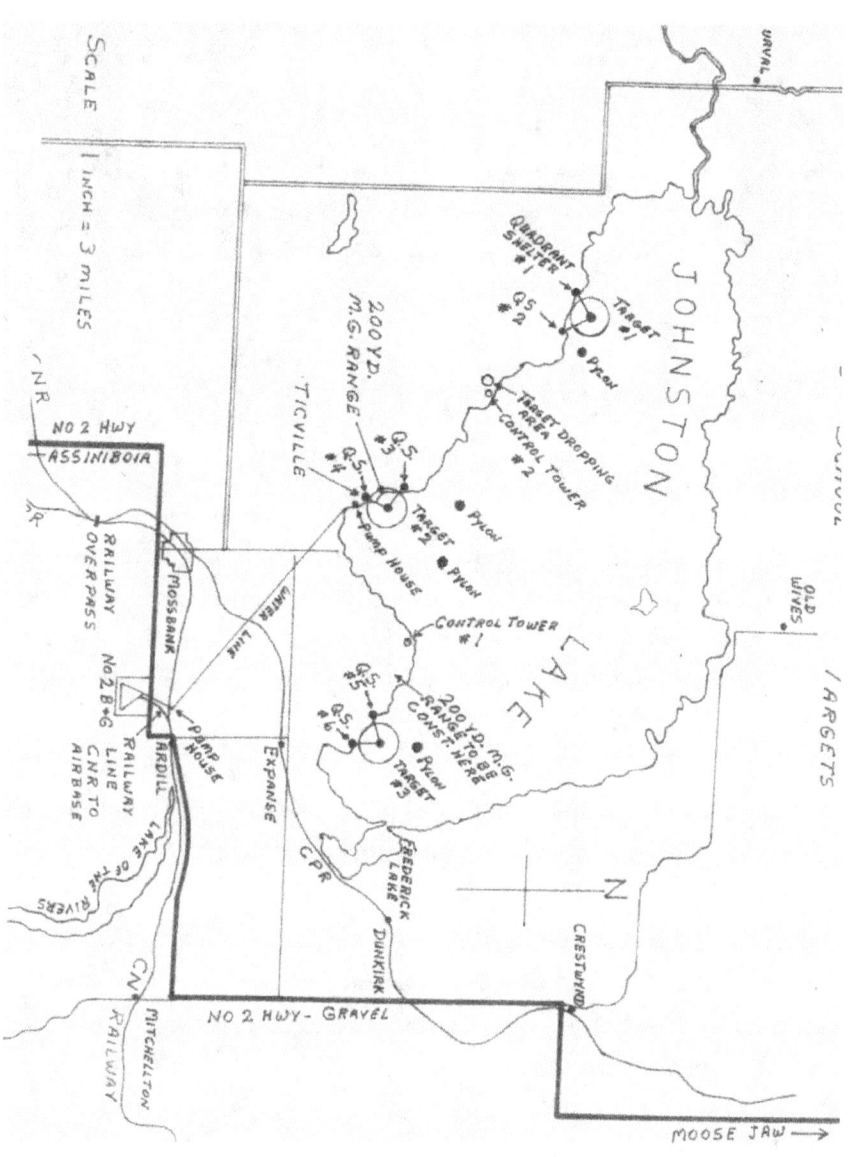

Lake Johnston Target Area

There were three bombing targets situated on Lake Johnston. The diagram on the previous page illustrates the location of the targets. There were two control towers along the shore, manned with observers.

The scale on the diagram of Lake Johnston is 1 inch equals 3 miles. The linear distance between the Control Towers was 39,600 feet.

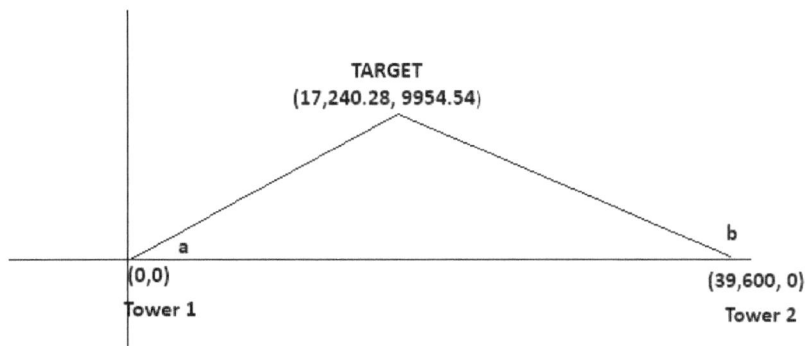

Cartesian Coordinates

To employ trigonometry, the position of the two towers and the location of the bomb target had to be laid out using Cartesian coordinates. Tower 1 had (x1,y1) coordinates of (0,0). Tower 2 had (x2,y2) coordinates of (39,600,0). Angle 'a' from the Lake Johnston diagram measured out at 30 degrees. Angle 'b' measured out at 156 degrees. The set of coordinates (x3,y3) was arrived at using the formula:

$$x3 = (39,600 \tan 156) / (\tan 156 - \tan 30) = 17,240.28 \text{ feet}$$
$$y3 = (39,600)(\tan 156)(\tan 30) / (\tan 156 - \tan 30) = 9,954.54 \text{ feet}.$$

Suppose a training aircraft was flying overhead and at the time the student's released bomb hits the water, the observer in Tower 1 records an angle 'a' of 30.2 degrees. Meanwhile over in Tower 2, the observer records an angle 'b' of 156.2 degrees.

The calculations for coordinates (x3,y3) reveal:

$$x3 = (39,600 \tan 156.2) / (\tan 156.2 - \tan 30.2) = 17,073.16 \text{ feet}$$
$$y3 = (39,600)(\tan 156.2)(\tan 30.2) /$$
$$(\tan 156.2 - \tan 30.2) = 9,936.58 \text{ feet.}$$

The student bomb aimer is off by 167.1 feet in the 'x' direction and off by 17.96 feet in the 'y' direction.

If these triangulation calculations seem daunting, think of how a student bomb aimer with only a Grade 12 education must have felt as he sat in the classroom listening to an instructor explore the finer points of trigonometry.

Despite the mathematical complexities, some bomb aimers were very skilled at hitting their targets as the following logbook entry attests.

October 3, 1941: Flying Officer F.S. Lapnewski, piloting Battle No. 1705 with LAC Eckert, A.J. as bomb aimer set a new Canadian record for low level bombing (2000 feet) when they dropped four bombs with an average error of only 17 and ¼ yards. Their record, however, was short lived as within an hour's-time Battle aircraft 1754 piloted by Sgt. G.A.B. Moore, and with LAC MacDonald, R.W. as bomb aimer, succeeded in dropping four bombs with an average error of only 16 and ¾ yards.

ACKNOWLEDGEMENTS

There are many who helped make this book possible. From those who planted the idea for the book in my mind, to those who helped me source research material. A heartfelt thank you to all of you!

To Barry and Dale Hicks of Hick Seeds Ltd. The idea for this book was sparked in September 2023 when you unexpectedly asked if I had ever thought about writing a book about the history of the Mossbank airbase.

To the archivists at the Provincial Archives of Saskatchewan. Thank you for your assistance in finding the many boxes of historical photos and documents.

To Joan Bumphrey and Bonnie Olafson at the Mossbank Museum. Thank you for sharing important research materials that helped in the development of this book.

To Donny Smith. Thank you for sharing your scrapbooks and wartime artifacts with me.

To Jeremy Patzer – MP for the Saskatchewan riding of Cypress Hills Grasslands. Thank you for the materials your staff in Ottawa provided as I wrote this book.

BOMBS AWAY!

NOTES

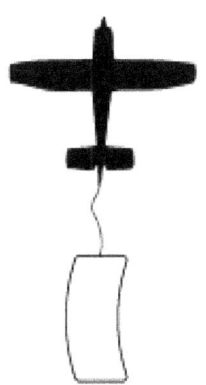

Chapter 1

Brill`s Encyclopedia of the First World War (2012). Edited by Gerhard Hirschfeld, Gerd Krumeich and Irina Renz. Leiden, USA.

Encyclopedia Britanica (2024). https://www.britannica.com/event/World-War-I/The-last-offensives-and-the-Allies-victory.

Encyclopedia Britannica (2024). https://www.britannica.com/event/Treaty-of-Versailles-1919/German-reparations-and-military-limitations.

Llewellyn, J. Thompson, S. (2023). *Russia in World War 1*. https://alphahistory.com/russianrevolution/world-war-1/.

MacMillan, M. (2013). *The War that Ended Peace*. Penguin Canada Books, Toronto, Canada.

National WWI Museum website (2024). *Armistice.* https://www.theworldwar.org/learn/about-wwi/armistice.

Norwich University website (2024). *Six Causes of World War 1.* https://online.norwich.edu/online/about/resource-library/six-causes-world-war.

Peters, M.S. (2017). *Bosnian Crisis.* https://encyclopedia.1914-1918-online.net/article/bosnian-crisis.

Top5sMedia (2017). *World War I: The War that Changed the World.* https://tubitv.com.

Chapter 2

Bernard, A. (2008). *20th Century History Review. The great Parisian world put to the test by the War.* https://shs.cairn.info/revue-vingtieme-siecle-revue-d-histoire-2008-3-page-13.

Bevans, C. (1969). *Treaties and Other International Agreements of the United States of America 1776-1949, volume 2.* U.S. Department of State.

Crafts, N. (2014). *Walking wounded: The British economy in the aftermath of World War I.* https://cepr.org/voxeu/columns/walking-wounded-british-economy-aftermath-world-war.

Encyclopedia Britanica (2024). https://www.britannica.com/event/World-War-I/The-last-offensives-and-the-Allies-victory.

Encyclopedia Britanica (2024). https://www.britannica.com/event/Treaty-of-Versailles-1919/German-reparations-and-military-limitations.

Heit, B. (2018). *The Death of Democracy.* Random Penguin House, Canada.

Le Bras, S, (2015). *Post War Economies – France.* https://encyclopedia.1914-1918-online.net/article/post-war-economies-france.

Llewellyn, J. Thompson, S. (2023). *Russia in World War I.* https://alphahistory.com/russianrevolution/world-war-1/

MacMillan, M. (2003). *Paris 1919.* Random House, Canada

National WWI Museum website (2024). *Armistice.* https://www.theworldwar.org/learn/about-wwi/armistice.

Norwich University website (2024). *Six Causes of World War I.* https://online.norwich.edu/online/about/resource-library/six-causes-world-war.

Peters, M.S. (2017). *Bosnian Crisis.* https://encyclopedia.1914-1918-online.net/article/bosnian-crisis.

Shirer, W. (1987). *The Rise and Fall of the Third Reich.* Bison Books, Hong Kong.

William-Jones, M. (2023). *2023 – The Crisis of German Democracy in the Year of Hitler's Putsch.* Basic Books, New York.

Chapter 3

Hitler, A. (1924). *Mein Kampf.* Translated by R. Manheim.

Shirer, W. (1987). *The Rise and Fall of the Third Reich.* Bison Books, Hong Kong.

Wexler, E. (2024). *Before He Rose to Power, Adolf Hitler Staged a Coup and Went to Prison.* https://www.smithsonianmag.com/history/adolf-hitler-coup-prison-beer-hall-putsch-180983207/

Chapter 4

Ferguson, N. (1999). *The Pity of War.* Penguin Group Publishing. London, U.K.

Shirer, W. (1987). *The Rise and Fall of the Third Reich.* Bison Books, Hong Kong.

William Jones, M. (2023). *1923 – The Crisis of German Democracy in the Year of Hitler's Putsch*. Basic Books, New York.

Chapter 5

Kershaw, I. (1991). *Hitler*. Longman Inc., New York, USA.

Shirer, W. (1987). *The Rise and Fall of the Third Reich*. Bison Books, Hong Kong.

William Jones, M. (2023). *1923 – The Crisis of German Democracy in the Year of Hitler's Putsch*. Basic Books, New York.

Chapter 6

Schmidt, Carl (1934). The Treaty of Versailles, Inflation and Stabilization. In: *German Business Cycles*, 1924-1933. Published by NBER. https://www.nber.org/system/files/chapters/c4933/c4933.pdf

US Office of the Historian website (2024). *The Dawes Plan, the Young Plan, German Reparations, and Inter-allied War Debts*. https://history.state.gov/milestones/1921-1936/dawes

Shirer, W. (1987). *The Rise and Fall of the Third Reich*. Bison Books, Hong Kong.

William Jones, M. (2023). *1923 – The Crisis of German Democracy in the Year of Hitler's Putsch*. Basic Books, New York.

Chapter 7

Hett, B. (2018). *The Death of Democracy*. Random Penguin House, Canada.

Hitler, A. (1924). *Mein Kampf*. Translated by R. Manheim.

Kershaw, I. (1991). *Hitler*. Longman Inc., New York, USA.

Schmidt, Carl (1934). The Treaty of Versailles, Inflation and Stabilization. In: *German Business Cycles*, 1924-1933. Published by NBER. https://www.nber.org/system/files/chapters/c4933/c4933.pdf.

Shirer, W. (1987). *The Rise and Fall of the Third Reich*. Bison Books, Hong Kong.

Wexler, E. (2024). *Before He Rose to Power, Adolf Hitler Staged a Coup and Went to Prison*. https://www.smithsonianmag.com/history/adolf-hitler-coup-prison-beer-hall-putsch-180983207.

William Jones, M. (2023). *1923 – The Crisis of German Democracy in the Year of Hitler's Putsch*. Basic Books, New York.

Chapter 8

Heit, B. (2018). *The Death of Democracy*. Random Penguin House, Canada.

Kershaw, I. (1991). *Hitler*. Longman Inc., New York, USA.

Shirer, W. (1987). *The Rise and Fall of the Third Reich*. Bison Books, Hong Kong.

Chapter 9

Bouverie T. (2019). *Appeasement – Chamberlain, Hitler, Churchill and the Road to War*. Penguin Random House, USA.

Dunmore, S. (1994). *Wings for Victory*. McClelland & Stewart, Canada.

Golley, J. (1993). *Aircrew Unlimited*. Butler & Tanner Ltd., United Kingdom.

Kershaw, I. (1991). *Hitler*. Longman Inc., New York, USA.

Chapter 10

House of Commons Debates, 18th Parliament, 2nd Session. February 16, 1937.

House of Commons Debates, 18th Parliament, 2nd Session. May 16, 1938.

House of Commons Debates, 18th Parliament, 4th Session. March 30, 1939.

Chapter 11

Kershaw, I. (1991). *Hitler*. Longman Inc., New York, USA.

Shirer, W. (1987). *The Rise and Fall of the Third Reich*. Bison Books, Hong Kong.

Chapter 12

House of Commons Debates, 18th Parliament, 5th Session. September 7, 1939.

Chapter 13

McCaffery, D. (1995). *Battlefields in the Air.* Lorimer and Company, Canada.

Canadian Museum of Immigration Pier 21 website (2025). *Anti-Semitic Exclusion and Canada's Immigration Policies.* https://pier21.ca/research/immigration-history/canada-and-ms-st-louis.

Change.org website (2025). *Erasing the Face of Former PM Mackenzie King from the Canadian $50 Bill.* https://www.change.org/p/justin-trudeau-erasing-the-face-of-former-pm-mackenzie-king-from-the-canadian-50-bill.

Hatch, F.J. (1983). *Aerodrome of Democracy.* Ministry of Supply and Services, Canada.

Chapter 14

Bouverie T. (2019). *Appeasement – Chamberlain, Hitler, Churchill and the Road to War.* Penguin Random House, USA.

Venville, M. (2024). *Churchill at War, Episode 2, Their Finest Hour,* Film Afrika Entertainment.

Chapter 15

Antonio, J. (2021). Air training program made Canada the 'aerodrome of democracy' during WWII. *Moose Jaw Today* (online) https://www.moosejawtoday.com/local-news/air-training-program-made-canada-the-aerodrome-of-democracy-during-wwii-4813291.

Black, D. (1989). *Skies Were Filled.* Published by Don Black, Regina, Sask.

Dunmore, S. (1994). *Wings for Victory.* McClelland & Stewart, Canada.

Hatch, F.J. (1983). *Aerodrome of Democracy.* Ministry of Supply and Services, Canada.

McCaffery, D. (1995). *Battlefields in the Air.* Lorimer and Company, Canada.

Chapter 16

PCL.com website (2025). *Our Story.* https://www.pcl.com/ca/en/who-we-are/our-history.

Images in this Chapter from: Saskatchewan Archives, Box F.745.445, 446, and 454.

RCAF Info website (2024). *RCAF Station Mossbank.* https://rcaf.info/rcaf-stations/Saskatchewan-rcaf-stations/rcaf-station-mossbank/#photo-gallery.

Chapter 17

Shirer, W. (1987). *The Rise and Fall of the Third Reich*. Bison Books, Hong Kong.

Chapter 18

RCAF Info website (2024). *RCAF Station Mossbank*. https://rcaf.info/rcaf-stations/Saskatchewan-rcaf-stations/rcaf-station-mossbank/#photo-gallery.

Saskatchewan Archives, Box F.745.445.

Mossbank and District Museum, Mossbank, Sask.

Chapter 19

RCAF Info website (2024). *RCAF Station Mossbank*. https://rcaf.info/rcaf-stations/Saskatchewan-rcaf-stations/rcaf-station-mossbank/#photo-gallery.

Saskatchewan Archives, Box F.745.452 and 455.

Mossbank and District Museum, Mossbank, Sask.

Zado, P. (1980). *Furrows and Faith – A history of Lake Johnston and Sutton RMs*. Friesen Printers, Manitoba.

Chapter 20

McCaffery, D. (1995). *Battlefields in the Air*. Lorimer and Company, Canada.

O'Malley, D. Vintage Wings of Canada website (2024). *Ghosts of Saskatchewan*. https://www.vintagewings.ca/stories/ghosts-of-saskatchewan.

Smith, E.G. (1942). Pact Gives Bigger Role to RCAF. *Globe & Mail*. June 6.

Chapter 21

Kritzwiser, K. (1942). Responsible Jobs Held By Airwomen. *Regina Leader Post.* June 1942. From the

Private Collection of Donny Smith – Mossbank, Sask.

RCAF Info website (2024). *RCAF Station Mossbank.* https://rcaf.info/rcaf-stations/Saskatchewan-rcaf-stations/rcaf-station-mossbank/#photo-gallery.

Saskatchewan Archives Box F 745.444, 453, and 454.

Chapter 22

ASME website (2000). *The Link Flight Trainer.* Available at: https://www.asme.org/

Our Own Devices YouTube Channel (2024). *WWII Practice Bombs: Training for Aerial Warfare.* Available at: https://youtu.be/MQyoqzi-E0w?si=FouAllFSbsRJUXvs

Saskatchewan Archives Box F 745.452 and 454.

Target (1944). Vol 4. No. 1. May 1944. p.6.

Target (1944). The Air Training of a Bomb Aimer. June 1944. pp. 36-37.

Private Collection of Donny Smith – Mossbank, Sask.

Chapter 23

RCAF Info website (2024). *RCAF Station Mossbank.* https://rcaf.info/rcaf-stations/Saskatchewan-rcaf-stations/rcaf-station-mossbank/#photo-gallery.

Saskatchewan Archives Box F 745.451 and 454.

Mowchenko Dam - photo courtesy of Mossbank area resident Dillon Ray.

Contact, July 1943

Chapter 24

Contact, November 1943

Target, April 1944

Two legacies were $96 and $304

Pole was 41 and 2/3 feet long

Coat worth $92

189.6 m.p.h

142 minutes

Chapter 25

Heritage Canada website (2024). *Royal Canadian Air Force operations record books* : C-12331. https://heritage.canadiana.ca/view/oocihm.lac_reel_c12331/1048.

Defense.gov website (2024). *D-Day: The Beaches.* https://dod.defense.gov/.

Chapter 26

RCAF Info website (2024). *RCAF Station Mossbank.* https://rcaf.info/rcaf-stations/Saskatchewan-rcaf-stations/rcaf-station-mossbank/#photo-gallery.

Saskatchewan Archives Box F 745.444.

Chapter 27

RCAF Info website (2024). *RCAF Station Mossbank.* https://rcaf.info/rcaf-stations/Saskatchewan-rcaf-stations/rcaf-station-mossbank/#photo-gallery.

Saskatchewan Archives Box F 745.444 and 453.

Chapter 28

Fox News website (2011). LIFE *Releases Previously Unseen Photos of Eva Braun, Adolf Hitler.* https://www.foxnews.com/world/life-releases-previously-unseen-photos-of-eva-braun-adolf-hitler

Douglas, W.A.B. (1986). *The Creation of a National Air Force.* Minister of Supply and Services Canada.

Chapter 29

RCAF Info website (2024). *RCAF Station Mossbank.* https://rcaf.info/rcaf-stations/Saskatchewan-rcaf-stations/rcaf-station-mossbank/#photo-gallery.

Saskatchewan Archives Box F 745.455.

Appendix 1

Canadian Aviation and Space Museum website (2024). https://www. Ingeniumcanada.org/aviation/artifact/fairey-battle-it.

Canadian Warplane Heritage Museum website (2024). https://www.warplane.com/aircraft/collection/details.aspx?aircraftId=65.

RCAF Info website (2024). *RCAF Station Mossbank.* https://rcaf.info/rcaf-stations/Saskatchewan-rcaf-stations/rcaf-station-mossbank/#photo-gallery.

Canadian Aviation History Society website (2000). Mossbank's wartime No. 2 Bombing & Gunnery School. https://sites.google.com/site/cahsreginachapter/mossbank-s-wartime-no-2-bombing-gunnery-school.

Hangar Flight Museum website (2025). *The History of the Avro Anson.* https://thehangarmuseum.ca/our-collections/avro-652-anson-mk-ii#

Canadian Aircraft Serials Personnel Information Resource (2024). 2 BGS- Bombing & Gunnery School (RCAF) https://caspir.warplane.com/perunitget/unitmiltype/RCAF_BGS/qd/2/

Saskatchewan Archives Box F 745.446, 447, 448, 449, 450, and 455.

Appendix 2

EugeneLeeSlover website (2025). *Naval Ordnance and Gunnery, Volume 2, Chapter 23, Aircraft Fire Control.* https://www.eugeneleeslover.com/USNAVY/CHAPTER-23-D.html

Map of Lake Johnston – courtesy of Mossbank resident Gregg Nagel

www.ingramcontent.com/pod-product-compliance
Lightning Source LLC
Chambersburg PA
CBHW071713120626
46550CB00001B/207

* 9 7 8 1 9 9 0 8 6 3 8 9 9 *